the
brower
quadrant

"Profoundly innovative and masterfully written, this philosophy stems from Lee's ability to learn from his experiences. *The Brower Quadrant* will awaken your true purpose and introduce you to dynamic systems that will enrich and sustain your True Wealth immediately and create a legacy that will have a life of its own.

John Gray
Author, *Men Are from Mars, Women Are from Venus*

"*The Brower Quadrant* is an absolute must-read for everyone, whether you are financially blessed or seeking to achieve financial freedom. Brower's experience and wisdom is elegantly presented through predictable systems that you can begin to use immediately. Lee Brower has created a brilliant blueprint for personal, family and business success that he so willingly shares."

Jack Canfield
Author, *Chicken Soup for the Soul* series

"*The Brower Quadrant* is a crowning rare jewel. Lee Brower's simple, yet provocative solutions to the age-old conflict between money and meaning is nothing short of transformational. This is a must-read for everyone, regardless of your current financial status. The principles in the book are so powerful that you cannot help referring to them constantly in your every day dealings with your family, friends and business associates. It will change the way you view life."

Lynne Twist
Author, *The Soul of Money*

"When we talk about success in life, money is always the first and sometimes only measure we have for it. Lee Brower shares an invaluable and comprehensive guide to Life 101. This compelling how-to resource effectively shatters traditional belief systems around wealth and prosperity and shares systems that contribute to meaningful, fulfilling life."

Ivan R. Misner, Ph.D.
Founder, Business Networks International (BNI)

"Using his experience and insights, Lee Brower has created a unique process called The Brower Quadrant. This process has many different dimensions, but the main impact is to transform families into positive forces for change in society. Instead of viewing money as a problem, Lee helps families see it as an opportunity for achieving happiness, meaning and significance."

Dan Sullivan

Founder, The Strategic Coach Inc.

"Lee Brower's contribution to the planet is his unique understanding of how to pass on True Wealth. He explodes the myth that the "goal" is efficiently bequeathing just our financial estate. In this ground-breaking book, Lee shares the four arenas of assets that, when synchronized, will not only create more meaning and more money in our lives now, but will assure that future generations thrive as well. He teaches with heart and deep wisdom.

Raymond Aaron

New York Times Top Ten Bestselling Author

thank
you

What is an acknowledgement?

... A sincere desire to say "thank you" to those who have contributed in some way to the completion of this book. Do I mention all those who over the years have inspired me? How about those who have encouraged me along my path of procrastination and desire for perfection? There are those who put in countless hours of editing, discussions, etc. And, there are all of the Quadrant Living Architects and Specialists and clients who have provided invaluable lessons from sharing their experiences.

My family! Thank you, Lori, for all that you do ... not just for the steadfast work on the book but for your unwavering positive influence and love that motivates and encourages me. And, to my children: Melody, a daughter and a mother who leads by example; Bo, a father, partner and champion; Nathan, an overachiever as a father and in his profession; Natalie, my inspiration; Stephanie, my sunshine. And, to Nick, who continues to overcome with his positive attitude; Carly, a believer that all things are possible; and Kelsey, who is an incredibly positive supporter. I love you and thank you!

At the risk of excluding some who have been extremely helpful and instrumental, let me name a few who have contributed directly or indirectly to the book:

My teammates: Paul Anderson, Brandon Newby, Melanie Davis, Dave Sheffield, Rick Bigelow and Jon McGowan. All of you have been a huge support.

My mentors: Dan Sullivan, John Wooden, Joe Bishop, and Jack Canfield ... Thank you!

My friends and colleagues at TLC (Transformational Leadership Council) ... Thank you!

My early supporters and co-creators Joel Baker, Ron Nakamoto, Bob and Beth Holt, Rick Demetriou, James Feek, Robert Keys, Michael Mathioudakis, David Parks, Kathy Peer, Donna Beers, James Priddy, Gary Thornhill, Marshall Thurber, Kip Kolson, Simon Singer, Jay Paterson, Douglas Andrew, Chuck Baldwin, Norm Bevan, Ken Guard, Victor Harbachow, Charles Hart, James Muir, Peter Tedstrom, Lee and Pia Jensen, Mary Beth Cameron and Matt Hadley.

And a special thank you goes out to the following individuals who, on very short notice and at their own expense, agreed to come and listen to me speak for an entire day to record my thoughts and provide clarity on the content for this book. Thank you so very much to:

Frank Alley	Brian Hardman
Stephanie Alsup	Robert House
MaryAnne Baker	Erik Johannessen
Jerry Bauer	James Johnson
Tom Boyd	Marilyn Johnson
Randy Bravo	Gary Kalus
John Bunge	Marshall Kalus
Clay Campbell	David Kawata
Diana Castro	Mark Klages
Rene Castro	William Knight
Miguel Chinea	Michael Levin
Arthur Cooper	Randall Lipsett
Cheryl Cooper	Barzel McKinney
Bo DeSimone	Dustin Morden
Donald Dimitruk	Mollie Voigt
Ryan Dunn	Mark O'Guinn
Eric Erickson	Christopher Oberg
Bryant Ford	Rick Parkes
Roger Gainer	Ann Marie Peterson
Glenda Golden	Jerry Quinn
Josh Golden	Debbie Ringchop

Tony Rodriguez
Dennis Scott
Bill Sefton
Daniel Spotts
Radon Stancil
Richard Thompson

the
brower
quadrant

live life deliberately

by lee brower

First Edition: April 2009
ISBN 978-1-481-11629-9
Printed in the United States of America

Book design by Brandon Newby

Visit our website at www.leebrower.com

table of contents

part one: developing the brower quadrant

1 What Is True Wealth? *3*
2 Money Talks, But Meaning Whispers *15*
3 The Brower Quadrant *27*

part two: understanding the brower quadrant

4 Core Assets *53*
5 Experience Assets *67*
6 Contribution Assets *87*
7 Financial Assets *109*

part three: the practice of quadrant living

8 Creating Clarity *133*
9 Gratitude Rocks! *159*
10 Goodbye, Goals *185*
11 The Empowered Quadrant Bank *209*
12 The Five Phases of Wealth *235*
13 Estate Planning Vs. Family Leadership *263*
14 Who Owns Your Future? *303*
15 The Essence of the Brower Quadrant *329*

partone
developing the brower quadrant

chapter 1

what is "true wealth?"

"The best season of your life lies ahead. No matter what your age or station in life—you have a choice. Ninety percent of your potential is not only untapped and unused, but also undiscovered."
Lee Brower

We often perceive money as the solution in our never-ending quest for peace and happiness. We give it unprecedented permission to set boundaries in our lives—in our work, our families and our relationships.

When we view our lives strictly in terms of our financial possessions, wealth comes at a high cost. We all know families that have been torn apart by money, and many of us know individuals whose lives might not include great financial abundance, but they are among the happiest people we know. They embody the expression, "When you're happy within, you can be happy without."

For the last thirty-three years, I've worked with some of the wealthiest individuals, entrepreneurs and families in the world. I've also worked with people deeply in debt and at virtually every level in between those extremes. Through that process, I discovered the real meaning of "True Wealth" and how to create it, grow it, manage it, optimize it, preserve it and pass it along intact to future generations. My discovery, The Brower Quadrant, is radical stuff that goes against what you know, but not what you have been taught about wealth.

I began working in the financial services industry fresh out of college. I was recruited by one of the largest planning firms in the United States. I was fortunate to work at the side of some of the finest estate and financial planners in the country, and through that experience I became fascinated with the estate planning industry. I couldn't learn fast enough. Friday mornings you could find me sitting in probate court taking notes, then meeting with attorney friends afterwards to get my questions answered.

As an advisor to the affluent, I began to examine whether the work I was doing—creating intellectual mechanisms for the rich to pass their wealth to their offspring without concomitant responsibilities—was one hundred percent beneficial. Was I protecting the wealth of hard-working people from the ravages of inflation, the IRS and other enemies of wealth preservation? Or was I, in effect, contributing to the delinquency of the generation of very wealthy heirs and trust-fund beneficiaries who would follow them? Was I helping my clients to be the best possible stewards of their wealth? Was I contributing to society or harming it?

I began to devote more and more time to studying some of the world's wealthiest families. I wanted to know why some families were successful in preserving wealth for generations, and why most family fortunes never made it to the fourth generation. According to the Family Firm Institute of Brookline, Massachusetts, "Nearly seventy percent of all family firms fail before reaching the second generation, and eighty-eight percent fail before the third generation; only a little more than three percent of all family enterprises survive to the fourth generation and beyond."

I was convinced that the reasons were not based on any financial secrets. I became obsessed with the idea of sustaining a family's wealth through four generations. If we could create a plan that would help a family sustain their most important assets through the fourth generation, wouldn't that increase the likelihood that these assets would survive far beyond that?

Thirty years of experience in the wealth-management field honed my skills at minimizing or even eliminating income, estate and inheritance taxes, but I noticed a highly disturbing trend: One might think that a family relieved of an unfairly heavy tax burden would be extremely happy, yet I discovered that no matter how much money I was able to save my clients, there was no correlation between their preserved financial wealth and their overall happiness. It bothered me that my work only helped my clients' financial picture, but did nothing to improve their level of happiness. If we in the financial services sector were so good at planning, why did financial wealth ultimately dissipate despite all our best efforts?

What's a Guy Like You Worth?

An incident that occurred several years ago gave me further insight. I found myself outside the door of a very young, affluent and influential CEO of a newly listed New York Stock Exchange company. I had been working with him and the company for several years, and I was there to pick up a very sizeable check. In fact, it would be the largest single check I had received up until that time. It represented a significant breakthrough for this young "almost" billionaire. His office was on the top floor of a ten-story building in which the firm occupied all ten floors. To say the office was opulent would be an understatement.

After waiting at least fifteen minutes beyond the appointed time, his secretary told me he was ready to see me. I entered through the large double doors and headed straight for the desk where Mr. CEO sat engrossed in the documents on his desk.

He looked up at me over the top of his glasses, and without any formal acknowledgement of my arrival, he lobbed a question at me that totally stopped me in my tracks.

"I've been wondering—what's a guy like you worth?"

What kind of question is that? I wondered. What does he mean, "a guy like you"? I had a pretty good idea of what *he* was worth. His stock in the company was public information and that was valued in excess of three quarters of a billion dollars. Not bad for a thirty six-year-old executive!

I don't know exactly why, but the question presented to me in that manner at that moment made the hair on the back of my neck stand straight up. I made every effort to maintain my composure, but I wasn't too successful.

I looked him straight in the eyes and with a firm (perhaps slightly quivering) voice said, "I will tell you what I'm worth. To my family, I am worth one heck of a lot! And while we're on the subject, let me tell you something else." (I now sensed I might be putting the forthcoming check at risk, but I continued.) "Some people are born downright ugly. Others are born with more serious handicaps; perhaps they're blind or crippled. Others experience tragedies during life that seem insurmountable or even unbearable. I don't believe that God cares as much about what happens to us as He does about how we *deal* with what happens to us." I took a deep breath, but I still couldn't hold back. "Perhaps your handicap is that you are rich! And I don't think God gives a squat how much money you have. What He cares about is what you do with it!"

You would have needed a butcher's knife to cut the tension in the room. I stood there becoming more fully cognizant of what I'd just said, expecting to be dismissed. Sweat seemed to be coming out of every pore in my body. After what seemed an eternity and a contest of wills, he quietly responded "You know, I was just thinking the same thing."

Whew! I walked out with the check in hand.

That incident forced me to examine the essence of everything I had been doing for the previous twenty years. I had been completely focused on money, investments, taxes and security, yet deep inside me there was this sinking feeling that I was missing the mark. That night, I wrote in my journal: What is my stewardship to wealth? And when does it end?

Thus, the quest for a new way of doing business began. I had come to the conclusion that my very profession was in many ways so focused on a person's net worth that the planning we were doing to preserve the financial assets had just the opposite result.

I'm pleased to confess that the young man with whom I met that day is currently regarded as one of the more charitable and responsible leaders in his community, and supports many wonderful causes throughout the world.

True Wealth

What is any one of us worth? Can we put a dollar value on what we are worth to our family and friends, to our business associates and clients? We are worth a great deal to our communities, as well, if we contribute of ourselves, financially or in other forms of service. In fact, the whole notion of worth expressed in dollars is utterly meaningless when we begin to think about how valuable we are to those around us, and how valuable they are to us. Are wealthy parents more beloved or more important to their children than middle-class or working-class parents? Of course not.

Many say that money makes the world go 'round, but only love can make time stand still. So the "worth" we have cannot be measured in financial terms. Someone once said that our true worth is what is left after the money is gone, and I believe it's worth repeating.

We have True Wealth when we enjoy financial abundance without neglecting our relationships, our communities or our personal searches for meaning. There are those—rich and poor—who have learned the secrets of True Wealth. They know that it encompasses things that money does not.

How do we balance the need for money and desire for wealth with our need for purpose and meaning? The answer lies within the question—*balance*. Balance demands we honor, develop and acquire symmetry between *all* of our assets:

Our *Core Assets* (the essence of who we are)

Our *Experience Assets* (the sum of our physical, emotional, mental, and spiritual experiences)

Our *Contribution Assets* (our effect on others)

Our *Financial Assets* (our net worth)

True Wealth comprises all of these assets; we don't want to sacrifice one for the other. Fortunately, we don't need to make that sacrifice. When we have True Wealth, we can maximize the enjoyment and benefit we receive from all of our assets. We can grow them, manage them, optimize them, preserve them, and pass them on to whomever we choose.

The Brower Quadrant System can help us define the "key" in each of our asset quadrants. After becoming familiar with the quadrants, and the aspects of our lives that they represent, we can use the examples in this book to gain clarity about the "Four Keys". These keys allow us to get into *quadrant* motion—optimizing our resources and creating more wealth *and* more meaning in all areas of our lives. Would you like to experience more wealth and more meaning?

As you read through this book, you will recognize the myths of traditional thinking as it relates to the acquisition, protection and utilization of your wealth, and understand why and how the current system of "estate planning" sets you and your family up for failure. What we call "Quadrant Living" can bring an experience of *clarity, balance, focus, confidence* and *predictability* into your life and the lives of those around you. By systematically employing all of your assets in your most important activities, you will be able to experience ever-increasing predictable results, and consequently, the benefits and blessings of True Wealth.

Quadrant Living enables you to focus on *your* unique ability and talents. This new focus will dramatically increase your accomplishments in those areas that are most meaningful to you. And finally, with increased clarity, balance and focus, your confidence will soar. Confidence is an attractant. It attracts great opportunities and great relationships. Aren't you attracted to confident people? Confident people attract. Those who lack confidence repel. The ability to instill confidence in others and to increase their confidence in you is vital to empowered achievement and happiness. It makes leaders out of each of us. The world needs your wisdom, accomplishments and leadership.

chapter 2

money talks, but meaning whispers

"This is our purpose: To make as meaningful as possible this life that has been bestowed upon us; to live in such a way that we may be proud of ourselves; to act in such a way that some part of us lives on."

Oswald Spengler
Historian/Philosopher

Here are three fascinating but little-known facts for your consideration:

1. In life, there's "True Wealth" and "False Wealth".

2. False Wealth is very seductive but has no real or lasting power.

3. True Wealth is one of the greatest powers on earth when harnessed and employed correctly.

The problem is, few people know the difference between True Wealth and False Wealth. It's not something we're taught in school or by most mentors, including our parents. As a result, so many of us end up aiming at the wrong target and unintentionally investing tremendous amounts of time, energy, effort and money into the pursuit of False Wealth.

How about you? Do you know the difference between True Wealth and False Wealth? Are you absolutely certain which target you've been aiming at?

The reality is ... "**Money talks!**"

For most people, the phrase "money talks" means wealth is power. The more money you have, the easier and better your life becomes. To a certain extent, it's true; money does solve many of life's problems, but there's more to it than that. Money sometimes lies. Money says: "Make the quest for me the most important thing in your life, and I will reward you with whatever you want."

Money may tell us that if we sacrifice our time and energy, or even friends, family, and health, money will reward us for putting it first. How many people do you know who make the accumulation of money their first priority, thinking that it will lead to happiness, peace of mind, and great relationships?

Has it worked? For most of us, a life of affluence sounds ideal. Only four percent of us have significant savings when we hit age sixty-five, and a majority of Americans have less than $1,000 in savings. More troubling, nearly one-fifth of us have a negative net worth, meaning that we owe more in debt than the total value of our combined assets. No wonder money fascinates us.

As I see it now, I was for many years *addicted* to working with only the very affluent. In fact, years ago, our business set a minimum of $25 million in net worth as a qualifying threshold for acquiring our services. Like many others, I wanted to be "around" affluence; I wanted to understand it, learn how to help others hang on to it, and create it for myself. I devoted 100 percent of my time to working with people whom I perceived had the greatest financial challenges and opportunities—the financially wealthy.

During that time, our firm commissioned a private study to determine the greatest fears that afflicted the affluent. The following are some of the issues identified through our study: What if I outlive my money or become obsessed with keeping it? What if my children are spoiled and never learn how to contribute to society? What if I can't make everyone happy? What if I never discover that "cause" bigger than self? What if I don't trust anyone? What if I spend my health to get all of this wealth and then lose the wealth trying to regain my health? What if I have so much going on, I forfeit the blessings of really knowing my family and friends?

Within the folds of all those dollars, an ever-growing vacuum can suck the purpose right out of life, leaving little but new worries, distractions and fears. Following are the top three fears of the affluent identified in our study. It is our subsequent experience that many at all levels of financial wealth possess these fears.

Fears of the Affluent

First: Loss of Choice and Control

Very simply, we do not want to give up control over our lives. We do not want to lose control over our health, our money, our assets, our relationships or our lifestyle choices. We will seldom deliberately give up control over our time, our money or our relationships without a fight.

We want to ensure that we do not outlive our income and thus become dependent on other family members or society in general. This is our greatest fear. The survey confirmed what we sensed intuitively: No matter how much money a family has, the family will still worry about losing control and independence.

Recent studies have shown the role that *control* plays in our happiness. In his book *Stumbling on Happiness*, Daniel Gilbert goes into great detail about the role *control* plays in determining our happiness and consequently affecting our longevity. He says that influencing things, changing things, and making things happen is a fundamental need with which human brains seem to be naturally endowed; and that much of our behavior from our infancy on is driven by our predilection for control.

Gilbert writes, "The fact is that human beings come into the world with a passion for control, they go out of the world the same way, and research suggests that if they lose their ability to control things at any point between their entrance and their exit, they become unhappy, helpless, hopeless, and depressed—and occasionally, dead."

So, this fear may be with us whether we are millionaires or paupers. The neutralizing action we can take is to develop systems to control what we can have control over. To do that we must first gain clarity about the assets we possess in all the areas of our lives, and then implement the systems that will optimize them over time.

Second: Possible Negative Outcomes ("Money will ruin our children.")

Lynne Twist, a world-renowned author, global activist, personal friend and colleague, states in her book, *The Soul of Money*: "Among families of great wealth, many have been poisoned by greed, mistrust and a desire to control others. Underlying most of this is a fear of loss. Their lives of privilege can cut them off from the essential experience of ordinary human interactions and authentic relationships." Family wholeness is one thing they will never be able to buy.

Some people say that money can ruin children. What do you say? Can money ruin our children?

I say: Absolutely not! I think you will agree that it is not the money itself; rather, it is the *ignorance* of money, the *misuse* of money, the *misunderstanding* of money, the *love* of money—or some combination of these things—that can "ruin" our children. Several stories in this book demonstrate that this does not have to be the case. Creating, preserving and transferring wealth in a meaningful way means passing on more than money; we also share our values, experience, knowledge, faith and other assets.

Recently, a father of seven and a very successful business owner confessed that eight years ago, he had lost his desire to make more money because he was afraid of what it could do to his family. He was a second generation welder who, after graduating from college, had joined the family business with his father in the family's garage. Blessed with the very unique ability to recognize bargains and opportunities and match them up, he increased the net worth of the company substantially. Having outgrown the garage and now occupying a large steel fabrication facility, he found himself questioning the potential cost of this burgeoning wealth. Was it worth risking the individual well-being of his wonderful family?

Eight years ago he was introduced to Brower Quadrant theories. Today, his company is a clear leader in his industry, thriving internationally. By most accounts, this is an impressive financial success story. However, he and his wife are most proud of how their family is unified in purpose as individuals who contribute to the strength and values of the family as well as society. They are contributors to society, intent on giving more than receiving.

Third: Not Leaving a Lasting Legacy

What is this life all about? Am I going to live and then die, soon be forgotten, or is there a way to leave something behind that will last beyond my lifetime? How can I make a difference?

Most of us don't want to be simply "successful"; we want to be *significant*. I believe that deep within everyone is the desire to have a passion bigger than self, to have the peace that comes from knowing that we are fulfilling our divine destiny, and knowing that we will leave the world a better place for others. How can we become high-impact individuals and families? How do we reach our God-given potential, and perhaps even exceed our own expectations for passionate personal achievement? Our research shows that the normal approach to estate planning used by lawyers, accountants, and insurance agents did little to address these fears, and in fact, often served to tear families apart. The way that money was handled—even the way it was thought about in the planning process—made enemies out of parents and children and pitted one child against another. This damage was often exacerbated by decades-old misunderstandings, conflicts and resentments about money and possessions that had grown up within these wealthy families.

I observed an immense desire on the part of these affluent wealth-creators to transform their families' attitudes toward money in creative and constructive ways. They really wanted to have their families intellectually, ethically and emotionally united. Their deepest desire was for *integration*. This desire, which I set out to satisfy while growing my business, is the concept that evolved into the Brower Quadrant system.

Meaning Whispers

Eventually, my "addiction" to working exclusively with the affluent came to a screeching halt. I attended a workshop in Toronto called BRAVO, a highly regarded public speaking clinic created by Teresa Easler. After spending three full days with a group of divergent industry leaders, I unexpectedly became the target of a full-fledged intervention: "Why are you ignoring the majority of the population? The theory of 'Quadrant Living' is for everyone," they said.

People from all walks of life and all levels of earning have fallen for money's lie; we've seen the disastrous results that so often accompany the decision to make money the priority—to the exclusion of many other important things. How many marriages, friendships and family relationships have been sacrificed at the altar of False Wealth? Somehow, many of us have ignored a critically important lesson: Yes, money talks, but money doesn't love us.

Meaning had been whispering to me, but it took the candid feedback of these workshop participants to bring me out of my denial. Soon after, we took the same concepts that we had successfully implemented with the very affluent and identified certain key principles within them that would benefit everyone. You will learn more about this in the following chapters.

Where's Your Wobble?

Think for a moment about a car trying to make its way down the highway with one tire over-inflated and three tires under-inflated. Would you expect a nice smooth ride?

That car is going to wobble almost out of control! Now, imagine that vehicle symbolizes the way you live your life. The financial aspect of our lives—earning, spending and investing money or possessing and maintaining things—represents one of the tires. The second tire has to do with who we are at our core: our beliefs and values, our families, health, talents and unique abilities. The third tire represents our experience: education, wisdom, life experiences, alliances, networks, reputation and skills. The fourth tire consists of our contributions motivated by gratitude: the areas in which we give back—not only with money, but also with time, energy, relationships and shared experiences.

For many of us, the vehicle makes its way down life's highway with one or more of our tires grossly over-inflated and the others under-inflated (perhaps even missing!).

Wouldn't it be great to equalize the pressure in each of our tires, so that we travel with a sense of balance? What would happen to the level of meaning and accomplishment in our lives if we were able to fully utilize the power of four fully inflated and balanced tires—our financial, core, experience and contribution tires? These are the four aspects of our lives that we will examine in the following chapters.

I predict that in these pages, you'll find a way to have wealth in all areas of your life—from a financial perspective, but also in the most important aspects of your life—from your core values to your life's experiences to your social and civic contributions. This is True Wealth.

chapter 3

the brower quadrant

"Wisdom is pure intelligence before the contamination of thought."
Sydney Banks, Author and Philosopher

When and where do you get your best ideas? While you're driving? In the middle of the night? If you're like me, they often come to you in the shower. I learned long ago that when I need an answer, I must first formulate a question. Once the question has been asked, the answer will come—it just doesn't come when I demand or expect it. In fact, it often comes when I least expect it.

I love the definition of wisdom proffered by the philosopher Sydney Banks: "*Wisdom is pure intelligence before the contamination of thought.*" You golfers, tell me, isn't that true? The more you think about the shot, the worse you do. For some reason, the reverse is also true. If you just go up there and hit the ball, staying in the moment—not caught up in thought—you often hit the perfect shot. This phenomenon is also evidenced in other sports; it's the basketball player who keeps his elbow in when he shoots without reminding himself to do so, or the baseball centerfielder who moves without thinking, even before the bat hits the ball.

As a financial advisor with extensive experience, I had long been asking certain questions: What is needed to acquire increasing wealth and maintain what you already have for yourself and future generations? Could we design a system that protected and empowered a family's True Wealth? How, exactly, do you add *power* to wealth?

A breakthrough came about ten years ago while showering before heading off to the airport to catch yet another flight, this time to see a client in Atlanta. Wisdom can be experienced in the shower, by having a great idea without even realizing you are thinking! Something magical happens when we cleanse our bodies—our minds get scrubbed, too, somehow. At least, that's how it was for me that morning in the shower. Like most great ideas, it didn't arrive while I was questing after it. I jumped out of the shower, toweled off quickly, dressed and promptly diagrammed the "Brower Quadrant."

As I headed to the airport, I couldn't let go of the concept; and, more important, it wouldn't let go of me. It just kept expanding, and gradually, I developed more clarity about the concept. As the idea continued to captivate me, I felt I had to share it with someone before I exploded.

On the flight to Atlanta, I sat next to a businesswoman who owned an art studio in Montana. I soon learned that she was an accomplished artist, that her husband was the property manager for one of the world's better-known entrepreneurs, and that they had two daughters. She asked what I did for a living.

As a result of my epiphany in the shower, I had an answer for her: "I optimize assets," I said confidently.

She looked both puzzled and intrigued. "Optimize assets," she repeated. "What exactly does that mean?"

I looked for a piece of paper so that I could sketch out the idea that had been building inside me all morning. In actuality, it had been developing much longer than that, but it had only come to conscious fruition in the previous few hours. I settled on the only thing I could find to write on: a paper napkin that the flight attendant had passed out.

"May I show you?" I began without waiting for an answer. I was delighted with the opportunity to test this clarifying interpretation on my unsuspecting neighbor. I began by writing the words "Optimize Assets" at the top of the napkin.

"When you hear the word 'assets'," I asked her, "what do you think of?"

My seatmate (whom I'll call Audrey) thought for a moment. "Well, I guess the first thing that comes to mind is ... money," she responded.

I wrote the word "money" on the napkin. "What other assets come to mind?"

Together, we made a list that included real estate, retirement plans, businesses, jewelry, art, stocks and bonds, and the like—*things*—assets typically itemized on our personal balance sheets. It looked something like figure 3-1 on the following page.

"Do you possess assets that you consider to be of greater worth than your Financial Assets?" I asked.

Audrey responded immediately. "Well, certainly," she said. "I would have to say my family."

"Great," I said, trying to hide my somewhat over-the-top excitement. "Let's call those types of assets our Core Assets because they really are at the heart of who we are." I wrote Core Assets in the center of the napkin.

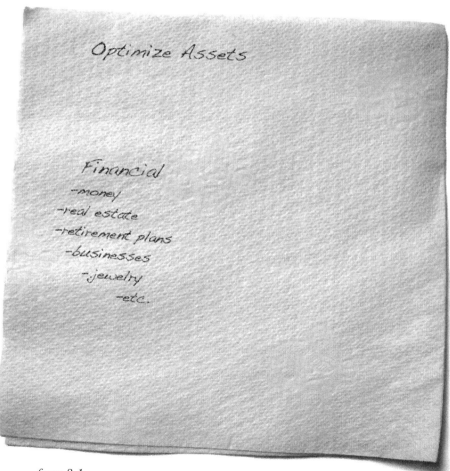

figure 3-1

"What other assets might we associate with our Core Assets? What about the health of each member of our family? Would you trade your health or the health of your loved ones for more Financial Assets?"

"Certainly not!" she exclaimed.

"What about the individual happiness and well-being of each family member? And what about your core values as a human being? Would you sell your values for more money?"

"I'm an artist," Audrey reminded me with a smile. "I would never compromise my values for anything."

Together, we added more items to the list of Core Assets. The list came to include our ethnic and religious heritage; our friends and other personal relationships; our unique abilities, talents and gifts (including her artistry); our spirituality and relationship with our God; and, of course, our *time*. The way we use our time today determines our future. So, one way to look at time is to think of it as our future. Whatever we do today is either a deposit or withdrawal from the bank of time that constitutes our future. My napkin now looked like figure 3-2.

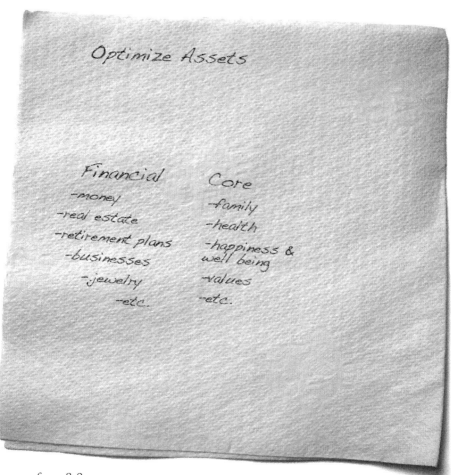

figure 3-2

"I'm enjoying this," Audrey said. "I've never looked at my assets this way before."

"To tell you the truth," I admitted, "I've never done this quite this way either. At least, not consciously. Okay, there is another category of assets to capture. Let's call these our Experience Assets." I wrote those words to the right of the Core Assets.

"Experience Assets," Audrey repeated, and I could see that she was a step ahead of me. "Obviously, the first thing that comes to mind is education."

"Agreed," I said, and wrote "Education" under the words "Experience Assets." "What else? What about life experiences?"

Audrey nodded. "Our experiences probably teach us more about life than anything else, including our education."

"Just our good experiences?" I asked.

She shook her head. "I've learned a lot more from my struggles than my successes," she said. "That sounds like a quote from somewhere, but it's definitely been true in my case. And, I guess not everybody learns from bad experiences because they keep repeating them. Then, they end up spending their time complaining rather than doing something with the knowledge they might have acquired had they been willing to learn from their experiences. I may not have *enjoyed* the bad times while I was going through them, but now, I'm so grateful for those experiences because they made me who I am—as a person and as an artist."

Next, we added our reputations to the list of Experience Assets. Certainly we wouldn't trade our reputations for more Financial Assets. We added to the list: alliances with others, networks, skills, methods, ideas and traditions. We looked at this rough diagram I had drawn on the airline napkin. I knew the artist sitting next to me was not especially impressed with my artwork, but I could see that the ideas definitely stimulated her thinking (see figure 3-3).

"As you look at this list, which categories of assets would you like to see carried forward into future generations?" I asked her.

She stared at the napkin for some time. "All of them," she said frankly. "I'd like our children and our future grandchildren to benefit from what my husband and I have acquired financially. But, I'd also like to see our Core Assets passed to future generations—our values, our heritage, our good health and well-being. And, of course,

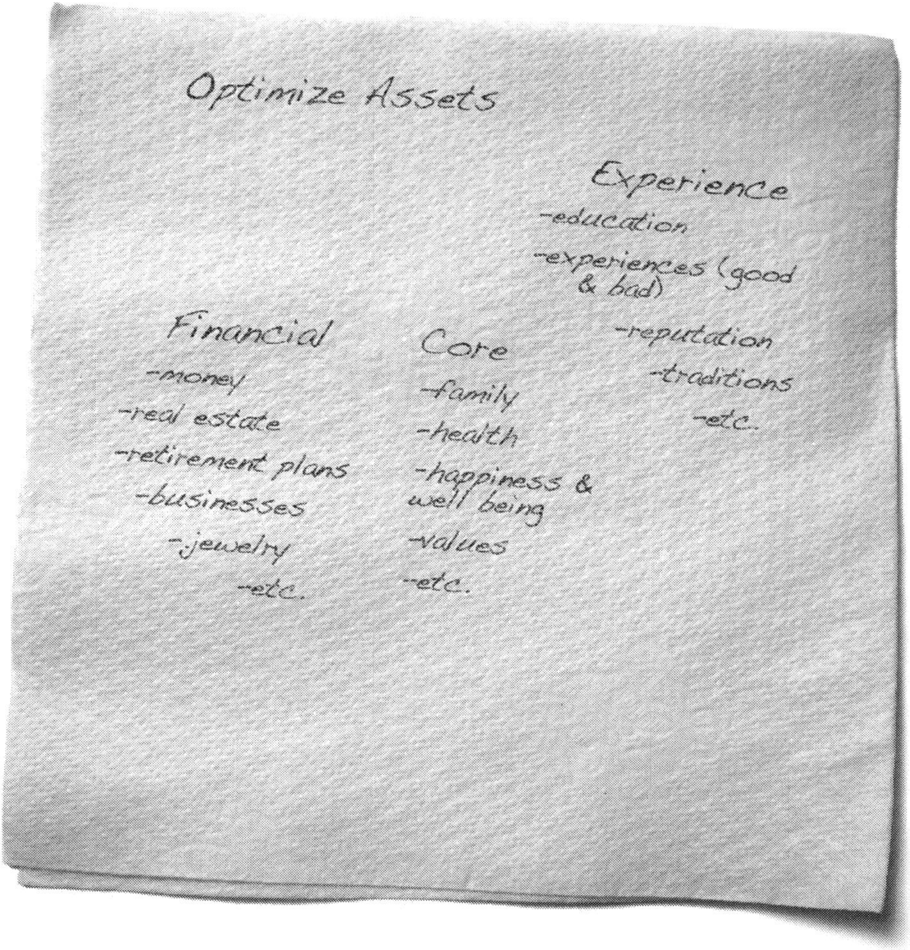

Optimize Assets

Experience
-education
-experiences (good
  & bad)

Financial
-money
-real estate
-retirement plans
-businesses
-jewelry
-etc.

Core
-family
-health
-happiness &
 well being
-values
-etc.

-reputation
-traditions
-etc.

figure 3-3

I want to carry on the tradition of formal education. If possible, I'd like to see our children and their children build on our experiences with new experiences of their own. I want our children to benefit from all the Experience Assets we wrote down here, including our reputation and our relationships."

Her answer was exactly what I had hoped it would be. "So you're saying that you'd like to see the best of *all* of your assets passed on to future generations, is that right?"

"Yes, of course," she said emphatically.

Now came the question that had occurred to me in the shower that morning. "Take your time and think it through carefully. If you could only transfer *two* of these asset categories to future generations, which *one* category would you leave behind? Financial, Core or Experience?"

How would you answer this question? If your children and grandchildren had to forgo one category of assets so they could fully benefit from the other two, which category would you forfeit?

After careful consideration, Audrey said, "I would leave the Financial behind."

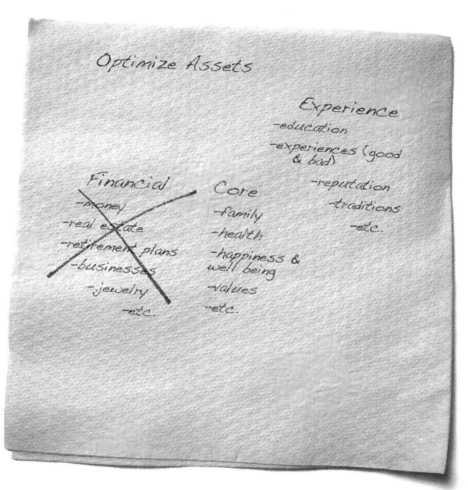

Optimize Assets

Experience
-education
-experiences (good & bad)
-reputation
-traditions
-etc.

Financial
-money
-real estate
-retirement plans
-businesses
-jewelry
-etc.

Core
-family
-health
-happiness & well being
-values
-etc.

figure 3-4

I have asked this question thousands of times to individuals, families and in front of large audiences. I always get the same answer.

Audrey gave the same reasons that thousands of others have given me since. "I know that if my children and their children are bankrupt in their Core and Experience Assets, the Financial Assets will eventually go away. I also know that if they are rich in their Core and Experience Assets, the Financial Assets will take care of themselves, and they will eventually thrive."

Wow! We both stared at the napkin. Why financial wealth rarely makes it through the second and third generations suddenly dawned on me. It has very little to do with all of the estate and financial planning we do.

Some individuals spend their entire lives building financial wealth and spend large amounts of time and money working to preserve that wealth for future generations. No doubt they have experienced the same epiphany I did. Do we spend most of our lives acquiring and protecting our earthly possessions, and way too little time *preparing* future generations?

"Okay," I said to Audrey, "let me ask you this—have you done your estate planning?" (I have since learned that this is a meaningless question; it is impossible to *do* your estate planning. But more about that later.)

"Yes," she replied. "Several times."

"And, where did you and your financial advisors focus your attention as it relates to the transfer of your assets to future generations?"

Again, she stared at the quadrants scribbled on the napkin in front of her, She knew the answer—the financial side of life, but there was a long pause before she answered. "Do we put things that matter most at the mercy of those things that matter the least?" she asked.

I responded, "Don't you find that remarkable? You just told me that if we would focus first on the northern quadrants—our Experience and Core Assets—the Financial Assets would take care of themselves. And yet the reason Financial Assets rarely survive the third generation is that *our society places emphasis on the wrong assets.* We get so caught up in the money game. On top of that, we don't have a system that focuses on the capture and enrichment of our Core and Experience Assets. Financial Assets are a means, not the end, when it comes to moving *all* of our assets to—and through—future generations."

Audrey nodded thoughtfully. "I'd like to ask you for something," she said.

"What's that?" I asked, surprised.

"I want that napkin!" she said with a broad smile.

"Wait, we're not done." There's still one more quadrant! The fourth quadrant—the lower right-hand side—is the quadrant of Contribution Assets. Contribution Assets are the assets we put back into society to do good things for its members. Our government has a name for these assets— they call them taxes.

"So, here's another question for you: Do most people consider taxes to be an asset or a liability?"

"I know my accountant puts taxes on the liability side of our financial statement," Audrey said.

"What if, starting immediately everyone on this plane was no longer required to pay taxes? How do you think most of us would feel?"

"You would have a plane full of ecstatic travelers." she said.

"There is a catch, however; from this time forward, we will no longer be able to benefit from any of the things taxes provide: roads, protection, medical care, education, schools, libraries, etc. Looking at it this way, perhaps most on board might rethink the value of paying taxes."

"Why, then, do we hate paying taxes?" she asked me.

"When we write a check to the Treasury on April 15th, when we pay our quarterly taxes or when we pay estate or inheritance taxes after a loved one passes away, we give up choice and *control* over those cash assets and how they are utilized. Honest Abe may have told us that this is a government by the people and for the people, but once we write a check to the government—unless we agree one hundred percent with the way the government spends our tax dollars—we have given up choice and control in a very significant way."

"How do we then regain choice and control over our Contribution Assets?" asked Aubry.

"The term I use is 'redirecting.' Believe it or not, the tax code gives us plenty of choices of how to redirect tax dollars back into society for causes we support and care about. We can redirect a portion of what we might other-wise pay in taxes, giving that money instead to charitable causes. We can accomplish this in a number of different ways, depending on our objectives and the nature and quantity of our Financial Assets. There are donor-advised funds and private foundations, or we can simply establish a 'proactive' Contribution Assets bank account and write checks to deserving organizations. These are several ways to accomplish the goal of redirecting our Contribution Assets, so that we regain choice and control over how that money is spent."

"I'm a Democrat," Audrey said. "I believe in paying taxes."

"I'm not opposed to contributing to society by paying taxes; I'm just against giving up choice and control. When you write a check to the government, your Financial Assets quadrant is affected. Every unnecessary dollar you take out of the bank and send to Uncle Sam is one less dollar that you control. I'll take it a step further; let's say that you have children and you want to educate them as to the importance of contribution because you want to develop their Contribution Assets. Would you rather write a check to the government to pay taxes, or redirect some of that money to a fund that your children could participate in, identifying and supporting causes they feel passionate about?"

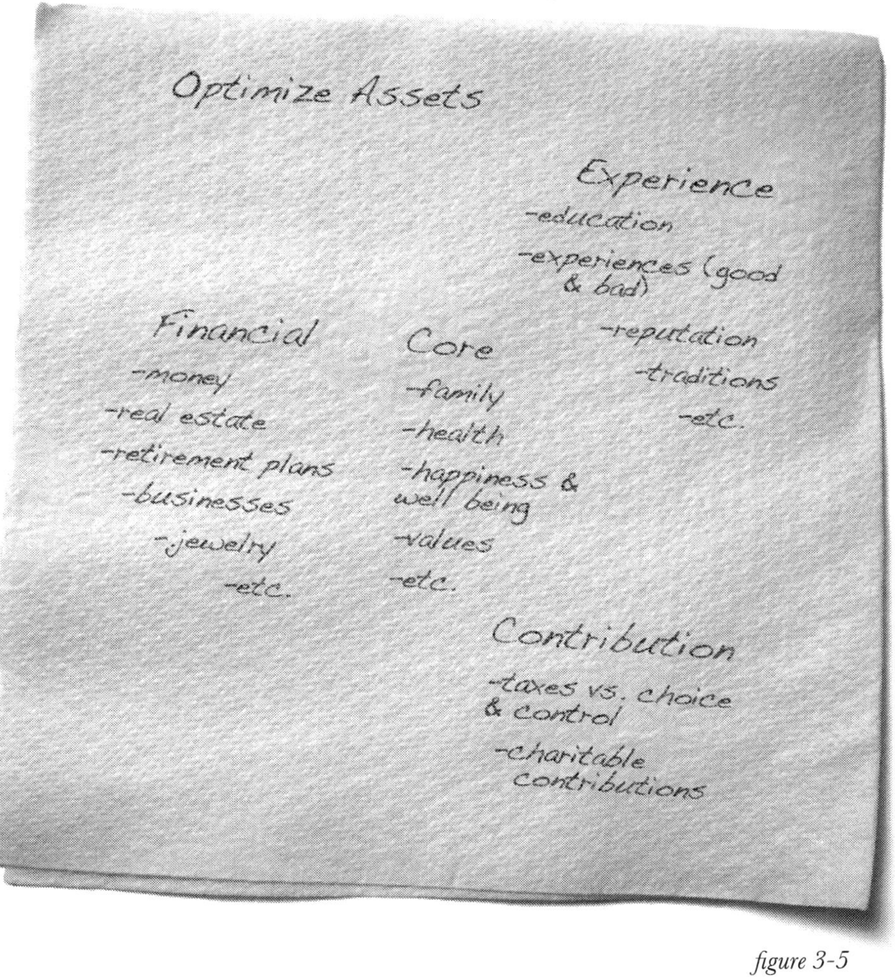

Optimize Assets

Experience
-education
-experiences (good & bad)

Financial
-money
-real estate
-retirement plans
-businesses
-jewelry
-etc.

Core
-family
-health
-happiness & well being
-values
-etc.

-reputation
-traditions
-etc.

Contribution
-taxes vs. choice & control
-charitable contributions

figure 3-5

"I have two daughters," Audrey said. "I'd love to see them involved in this kind of decision-making."

"We choose our charitable organizations based on our own core values. If we were to ask our children to focus on their core values and thus determine what charities would mean the most to them, we would be helping them develop their Core Assets as they evaluate and make contributions.

"At the same time, if we ask them to educate themselves about these charities, about the needs of society and about which charity might be best at meeting a given need, we are developing our children's Experience Assets—part of the Experience quadrant. In sum, every dollar that we proactively redirect from taxes—thereby regaining choice and control—affects our Financial Assets, as well as our Core and Experience Assets, and those of our children, while simultaneously doing good for our favorite causes."

"I get it," Audrey said. "And, I sense that the four quadrants work even more powerfully when you consider them together instead of separately."

"Exactly. As the saying goes, 'the whole is often greater than the sum of its parts'. When you begin to look at life in terms of your family's unique Core, Experience,

Contribution and Financial Assets, it quickly becomes apparent that the sum of the whole of these assets is worth far more than the constituent parts. I call this added level of success and power *Quadrant Intelligence.* It reaches its optimum level when a family integrates all four forms of assets. When this happens, the family thrives in undreamt of, and even miraculous, ways."

I then took my pen and circled each Asset category in one continuous motion, integrating the Core Asset as the heart of the Brower Quadrant. "Each quadrant is dynamic in its own element, synergistically connected with one another, driven by the Core, to represent our True Wealth."

Audrey grinned. "Now, can I have the napkin?"

"Now you can have the napkin," I said.

The Brower Quadrant

That morning was the birth of the Brower Quadrant. I now felt I could share with others a means by which all of our assets—not just material wealth—could be transmitted to those in our circle of influence: our spouses, our children, our extended families, our businesses, our communities and our world.

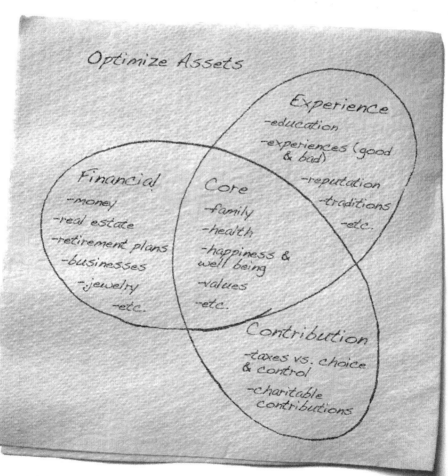

figure 3-6

Countless families today utilize the Brower Quadrant as their lodestar to experience "Quadrant Living", a system for capturing all of the varied assets that families possess, living by them and sharing them with future generations.

Sometimes people say to me, "Lee, when I'm rich, I'll be thrilled to put the Brower Quadrant into my life. Until then, I can't afford it."

They've got it backwards. Our research indicates that you can employ the Brower Quadrant at any time, no matter how much or how little your family has in the bank. As mentioned earlier, money is a primary concern for all of us, sometimes to the exclusion of all of the other values captured by the Brower Quadrant. When we emphasize one quadrant to the exclusion of another, we are maneuvering through the challenges and opportunities of life on one over-inflated tire and perhaps three less than optimally inflated tires. One or more tires may actually be flat. It doesn't matter whether it is the financial tire or one of the others; without the balance, we will have a wobbly vehicle. We will lack focus, balance, velocity—and therefore, confidence.

What if we were to "pump up" our attention to those other three quadrants? What if we paid equal attention to each? Does that mean we have to spend equal time in each quadrant?

Different areas of our lives require different levels of attention and focus depending on our circumstances at that moment. A wobbly vehicle means that we need to check the tires daily. Check the air in each tire (quadrant) and then focus on those activities that will generate the greatest result without the wobble slowing you down. We can enjoy a new level of balance, velocity and effectiveness in every aspect of our lives. And the same will begin to occur for those in our circle of influence.

The remarkable thing that you will discover is that the more you pursue meaning in your life, the more money ends up pursuing you.

parttwo
understanding the brower quadrant

chapter 4

core assets

"Make the most of yourself, for that is all there is of you."
Ralph Waldo Emerson

What's more important than your own health, happiness and well-being? The Core Assets quadrant contains those assets you value most: your family, your health, your spirituality and sustaining beliefs, your uniqueness and your God-given talents.

Core Assets influence every other quadrant. The Brower Quadrant logo was designed with the Core quadrant in the center to reflect this idea. All of the quadrants operate synergistically, meshing with other quadrants, but the Core quadrant is at the heart of the system. If left with only one quadrant, most would choose their Core Assets.

Is there anyone else exactly like you? When Reverend Jesse Jackson addressed the 1984 Democratic National Convention, he used a phrase to define himself at the core level. The phrase was: "The me that makes me *me*."

The you that makes you *you* symbolizes and summarizes your Core Assets. These are intrinsic—you're born with

or into them. Your responsibility is to nurture them, allow them to grow and expand to their potential: Your family, your health, your values and, of course, your unique abilities and talents. These are the abilities, tendencies and proclivities with which we were endowed at birth.

I was fortunate enough to attend a small dinner gathering hosted by Warren Buffet, who was asked to what he attributed his success. "Two things," he immediately responded. "First, I was born with a natural instinct to recognize capital market opportunities. I don't know why, I just know that it has always been easy and enjoyable. "And second, I was born in the United States of America, a country that allows me the freedom to employ that unique ability. The combination of those two things has allowed me to approach my potential."

For Mr. Buffet, unique ability and freedom were two very important Core Assets. These special unique abilities or talents are gifts. They come to us without having to ask for them. They simply arrive as part of our DNA when we appear on the planet.

To whom much is given, much is expected. "For unto whomsoever much is given, of him shall be much required." *The Holy Bible, King James Version*, Luke 12:48. The price of a gift is that we make full use of it.

But do we? Everyone has a unique ability, a way of being in the world, a way of serving others, a way of creating, performing or discovering that is truly his or her own. But the requirements of day-to-day life—earning a living, meeting our family responsibilities—more often than not, conspire to rob us of the time that we could invest in making full use of our unique abilities.

Few of us have actually determined what our intrinsic gifts really are. Those who know what they are capable of often fail to act on their gifts, often out of fear (of both failure *and* success). They have been conditioned not to "stand out from the crowd." And yet, at our core, we possess great gifts—our unique method of bringing value to those around us.

The vision for your unique ability is this: You are able to devote ever-increasing amounts of time to *living in your unique ability* while finding ways to delegate, or minimize, those aspects of your life that do not truly serve you or those around you. When you get in touch with the you that makes you *you*, when you are acting out of your unique ability, you experience a sense of flow and timelessness that brings a deep feeling of joy. I carry with me the following quote from Marianne Williamson's book, *A Return to Love*:

Our deepest fear is not that we are inadequate. Our deepest fear is that we are powerful beyond measure. It is our light, not our darkness, which frightens us. We ask ourselves, who am I to be brilliant, gorgeous, talented, fabulous? Actually, who are you *not* to be? You are a child of God. Your playing small doesn't serve the world. There's nothing enlightened about shrinking so that other people won't feel insecure around you. We are all meant to shine, as children do. We were born to make manifest the glory of God that is within us. It's not just in some of us; it's in everyone. And as we let our own light shine, we unconsciously give other people permission to do the same. As we're liberated from our own fear, our presence automatically liberates others.

It is not enough just to live, just to survive. It is imperative for each of us to equip ourselves to abundantly contribute to society—to acquire more and more "light," so that our personal light can help illuminate a darkened world.

In *The Road Less Traveled*, M. Scott Peck defines unique ability as *cathexis*, a state in which we "cathect," or break down the walls between ourselves and the thing we love to do or the person with whom we love to be. We achieve this sublime state of cathexis when we are doing the thing we love the most—be it working on our rose garden, playing the piano, writing, putting together business deals, finding new ways to serve our religious institution, or putting a beautiful meal together in the kitchen. As time passes, we find different "delivery systems" for sharing our unique ability with the world. We find new ways to cathect, and in so doing, we experience "the us that makes us *us.*"

Identify Your Core Assets

When we talk about the search for Core Assets, we focus on our individual health, happiness and well being:

What do I love to do so much that I would do it if nobody paid me to do it?

What makes me happiest?

Where do I maximize the amount of joy in my life, and, not coincidentally, where do I bring the most service and joy to others? This is perhaps the most overlooked Core Asset that you possess—the unique gift bestowed upon you that you, in turn, have the privilege of sharing with the world.

This is only the beginning of our Core Assets. Family members and personal friends are Core Assets. These are the people who will stand by us, the people with whom we share our greatest triumphs and tragedies, the people who are "there for us." We don't choose our families, but we do choose that circle of friends, mentors and go-to people who help us get through the tough times and with whom we share our transcendent moments. We are wired to want to be with others, to form bonds of love and security. It's part of our nature, and we honor it when we take time to recognize the depth of the relationships we are privileged to create. Family and friends constitute a vital Core Asset.

The same is true of our heritage. The beautiful thing about our society is the freedom we have to honor and celebrate commonalities and differences. The me that makes me *me* may well be entirely different from the you that makes you *you*—and yet we don't have to prove to each other that one heritage or culture is better than the other. This sense of acceptance is part of what makes America great. Our ethnic and religious heritage, combined with our national heritage, constitutes yet another vital Core Asset.

The same can be said of our religious faith and our approach to spirituality. This Core Asset has no value if it lies dormant. We need to *live* our spiritual values and not keep them tucked away in a drawer. The quadrants provide a framework to help individuals and families apply spiritual values to day-to-day activities. The Brower Quadrant helps us see the big picture. Before we do anything, we must ask, "Is this in line with my values?" And when we say values, we mean positive values—our virtues.

Our health is a Core Asset that is often all too easily overlooked until it diminishes. Our health is probably the Core Asset that we value the least—until it suffers. We use our health to get wealth, and then, as we get older, we spend our wealth to improve our health. As William George Jordan wrote in *The Majesty of Calmness*, "In the race for wealth, men often sacrifice time, energy, health, home, happiness, and honor—everything that money cannot buy, the very things that money can never bring back."

Frequently, when I am explaining the Brower Quadrant (or presenting the "Napkin Presentation"), I ask the participants if they would trade their family, health or values for more Financial Assets. I have yet to meet anyone who would seriously consider that exchange. Yet, how often does each one of us make that trade? Do we not at times trade our time and attention with family so that we can make more money? How about our health? Do we not sometimes sacrifice health for the almighty dollar? And values—all we have to do is look in the newspaper every day and we see reports of executives who did only one thing wrong in their eyes—they got caught. One definition of rationalization is the lowering of our standards to meet the level of our behavior. We can justify our neglect of family, health or values if we rationalize that our efforts will someday make us all more happy, healthy and wealthy.

Virtue-Based Values

Values are intrinsic to every outcome. We all have values, but not all values are virtuous. Actions demonstrate our values. Hitler had values, but they were certainly not virtuous values. We are painfully aware of those misguided values. What needs to be uncovered and nourished are virtue-based values. These are the values that extend and reinforce the bridges that allow the transportation of all of our assets of great worth to future generations. When virtue-based values are reinforced by traditions and ceremonies, they become part of the fiber that makes up the mosaic of the entire family. The focus can then center on the true assets of greatest worth—those with tremendous staying power for generations to come.

With the practice of ceremonies and traditions, individuals attain and carry a higher sense of worth and purpose, reinforced by the sense that *together we are better*. Decision-making becomes easier. A virtue-based purpose that is supported by the family allows for better decision-making.

You become *proactive* rather than *reactive* because you know your desired outcome.

Taking the time to dig deep to unearth your true values and committing them to writing is essential. Living in an environment that echoes your identity and purpose is the security blanket of life. You feel at home; and there is peace, safety and security—a refuge from the world.

Happiness is yet another example of a Core Asset frequently ignored or overlooked. I define happiness as *peace of mind*. Retired American basketball coach John Wooden defines it this way: "[Happiness is] knowing that you've done all that you're capable of doing to achieve all that you're capable of achieving." It's not about beating the other guy, and it's not about titles, victories, banners or trophies. Rather, happiness comes from knowing that we have given our all. Researchers at the University of Michigan recently looked into the question of what makes people happy. Their research produced some interesting results. First, people pay a great deal of attention—perhaps too much—to the immediate events in their lives, good or bad, instead of looking at the big picture. People tend to say that they're happy if good events have happened in the last week or so, and unhappy if the reverse is true, without considering the "big picture" of their whole lives. They tend to discount even the Core Assets that we've discussed, and instead put too much importance on the "headlines" in their lives. This means, the researchers concluded, that people tend to make their happiness contingent upon getting good news, which, of course, is something out of our control. The research confirms that if people focus on the simple joys of life—spending time with close friends or even getting a good night's sleep—they are much happier.

The University of Michigan research also determined that we as a society are not happier than we were a generation or two ago, despite the great advances in material goods and technology. We aren't even happier than people who have less. It turns out that the happiest, most hopeful people in the world aren't those with the most material wealth. Surprisingly, according to this research, the happiest people in the world reside in Africa. How could that be? How could people in dire economic straits be happier than the typical middle-class American?

If we hold our happiness hostage to good news, who controls our future? Is it controlled by us or by the events happening around us? Clearly, we aren't in control of our happiness if we are waiting to find out what's going to happen next. And yet, we do it all the time. It's almost as though we are paying too much attention to the weather and not enough to the climate. Yes, there are going to be some rainy days in all of our lives. Does this mean we should postpone happiness until the sun comes out? The weather is beyond our control. Outside events, by definition, are beyond our control. Yet our mindset—the way we react or respond to life—is entirely within our purview.

Who is in control of your future? If you are, it's because you have mastered the art of focusing on your vision and the ways in which *all* of your assets are critical in achieving that vision. You don't allow the complexities of day-to-day life to take you up too high or down too low—this is balance. If outside events dictate your mood, buckle up. It's going to be a bumpy ride.

You are more than the last piece of news you received—good or bad. It's also worth remembering that as we go through our lives, we are not always the best judges of whether something that happens to us is inherently good or bad. Sometimes a breakdown is a breakthrough. When Bill Gates quit Harvard, his parents must have been distressed. Do you think they would be disappointed now? Sometimes an individual escapes an abusive marriage, goes through the pain of divorce and then readies himself or herself for a new and beautiful relationship. A business failure teaches an individual to redouble his efforts, to work harder and smarter, and an otherwise unattainable level of success becomes reality.

Celebrate the "you that makes you *you.*" Your Core Assets are different from everyone else's on the planet. This means that the contribution you offer the world is as unique as you are, and nothing could be more exciting than that.

How would you describe the "you that makes you *you*"?

What are your unique abilities?

What are the unique abilities of your family members?

What are your virtue-based values?

chapter 5

experience assets

*Instead of life dictating its
terms, you are choosing what is
remembered, what matters, and
what will be available to future
generations.*

Who owns your past?
Is it an asset or a liability?

For some it is a liability. They can't seem to get out of the past and into the present. They lean on the "good ole days" for their glory. Others live as victims, blaming conditions today on their experiences in the past. They cannot let go of grudges, resentments or other remnants of previous experiences. Isn't our past just a collection of thoughts? If they are thoughts, can't they be changed instantly? Millions of dollars are spent each year on what some refer to as "traditional" clinical therapy. Although this may be necessary for some, many times patients are encouraged to re-live the past ad infinitum. Perhaps these therapists measure their success by the number of tissues consumed during a session?

The philosopher Sydney Banks contends that a memory is a thought carried through time. "There are good memories and bad memories. If you have a good memory, it's beautiful. It's not a *reality* any more, but it's beautiful. I have good memories of my past ... and sometimes when these memories come into my head, it's a beautiful feeling, and I accept it. I accept it as an illusion. I accept it because it's nice. Now, if a bad memory comes in, I know it's an illusion, and I just drop it because—it's now non-existent."

Your reality comes from the inside out, and once you realize that, your reality changes. When you change your thoughts, your reality changes. You have probably been in a bad mood and thought the world out there looks crummy; your wife looks terrible, your husband looks terrible and your dog's a pain in the rear end. Everything's going wrong. Then, something happens, your consciousness rises, you *change* your thoughts, and you say, "Oh honey, you're beautiful, I love you, and hey, isn't that a sweet little dog we've got?"

The dog's not changing; your partner's not changing. It's your *thoughts* that are changing. If you feel sad, you have negative thoughts, and you can change them from negative to positive. I'm simply reminding you that these thoughts are an illusion; you are in a position to make a choice—you can *choose* the happy thoughts, if you are aware of your ability to choose.

For some, past experiences, regardless of whether they are good or bad, are assets because these people continue to learn from them. Dan Sullivan, co-author of *The*

Laws of Lifetime Growth: Always Make Your Future Bigger Than Your Past, writes "Always make your learning greater than your experience." All experiences are potential assets. This approach encourages good thoughts, and good thoughts attract positive outcomes. When we hang on to negative thoughts, we actually feed that negativity and attract to ourselves the very things we despise.

Life's lessons come in many ways and from many sources. Sometimes we travel a long way to learn something important. This was the case for me when I found myself in Ulan Bator, Mongolia with my son Bo on a hunting trip. When I purchased the trip in a charity auction at a Boy Scouts of America dinner, I had no idea that this expedition would offer me one of the most important insights I would ever acquire.

Traveling to Ulan Bator is no easy matter, especially when you're carrying large amounts of children's medication, which Bo and I were attempting to smuggle through China to help the children of Ulan Bator. We had carefully placed the medicine between eighty homemade quilts that we were taking to an orphanage, as well as checking through our hunting rifles and ammunition. Proceeding through Beijing Airport and on to Ulan Bator, before customs could make too careful a search of our belongings, was paramount. Luck was against us, however. An unexpected snowstorm shut down the Beijing airport, and as a result, we had to spend an unplanned night in Shanghai. That turned out okay because our bags remained with the plane. The dilemma was that if we missed our connection—the only weekly flight from Beijing to Ulan Bator—we would have to clear customs and spend an additional night before proceeding to Mongolia (on Mongolian Air, whose fleet consisted of *one* plane—a gift from North Korea).

As we approached the armed custom agents, I asked Bo if he was nervous. He was a 16-year-old junior in high school. He confessed that he wasn't.

"Why should I worry? I'm with you, Dad."

Dad, meanwhile, had sweat rings down to his waist. Miraculously, the customs agents in Beijing did not look through our bags, but what we had hoped would be a standard connection stretched into a twenty-four-hour delay. We spent a very nervous day and night with the medicine and weapons before we were finally able to board a jet for the final leg of our journey.

Neither the mission of mercy—taking the medical supplies to the Mongolian physicians—nor the hunting turned out to be the most important event of the trip for me. For

Bo, the delivery of the quilts was a very meaningful and emotional experience. But for me, my life-changing experience took place at the Mongolian Stock Exchange—the brainchild of a 28-year-old Mongolian gentleman who went by the nickname of Zolo.

The winds of freedom had reached even far-off Mongolia, and young Zolo had conceived the idea for a stock market where investors could trade shares of ventures, just as the rest of the world does. Zolo took great pride in his creation and told us that he frequently led tours for school children, journalists and anyone else interested in seeing one of the first harbingers of free enterprise to reach this formerly Communist nation. He shared with us the long hours he put in, sometimes working well past midnight. He told of students lined up outside the doors to learn about democracy and the free enterprise system. They were starving for knowledge.

Zolo's front teeth were chipped. When we spoke about his motivation to work so hard and his devotion to sharing, the conversation turned to what had happened to his teeth. He explained ruefully that the damage was a result of his honest opinion about the state of the Mongolian economy.

Local government officials now had to compete in free elections for their seats, a novel experience after decades of Communist rule. These Communist leaders frequently made television appearances during the campaign in which they assured the nation that the economy was doing great. Zolo knew otherwise, and shared his opinions about the realities of Mongolia's struggling economy with a journalist. After the interview appeared in a local newspaper, Zolo was arrested and brought down to City Hall for a traditional Communist-style interrogation. That's when he suffered the damage to his teeth.

Zolo bore the memory stoically. The next words he spoke electrified me, and as a result, changed my life. "I realized in a flash," he said, after describing the beating, "that everything I possessed could be taken from me—my house, my car, my money. It could all be gone in a flash. But what I have in here"—he tapped his head—"can never be taken from me."

I was elbowing my son. Was he listening? A typical American teenager, he was focused on football and girls. Education was something he had to do, not something he hungered for. For years, I thought *this* was the message. Bo and I talked about the importance of education and the worth of knowledge. It was the lesson we needed to share at that time.

Then, about three years later, I was reading Zolo's account in my journal. Thank goodness for my journal. (Someone once said that a dull pencil is better than a sharp mind.) I had no memory of what Zolo had said when pointing to his head and saying, "... what I have in here can never be taken from me."

I found what followed even more profound: "What I have in here is of no value to anyone except me. When I die, it will die with me—unless I give it away. When I give it away, it has a life of its own!" A still voice within told me this was incredibly important.

Zolo's stock exchange existed in order to capitalize assets— to create value by allowing people to benefit from the experience, wisdom and hard work of others. Re-reading Zolo's words, I realized that he was doing the very same thing with his life experience—the assets or memories in his head. He had recognized—and was teaching me—that the knowledge and experiences we hold in our brains are vitally important assets. But to capitalize that asset-to increase its value—we must give it a life of its own. And to do that, we must first capture the experience in writing or verbally share it with others. If we die without sharing those assets with others, the value of our Experience Assets dies as well.

Have your financial advisors ever recommended you to invest for your future by investing your hard-earned dollars in the space under your mattress? Is this the kind of recommendation you would receive from the best financial advisors? Why would you *not* receive this advice? They, and you, know the reason. This financial asset— your investment dollars—would not be working for you. They would become idle assets depreciating in value with each passing moment.

So what about our Experience Assets? If we value them as much as or more than our Financial Assets, are we guilty of investing those assets under our mattresses and not putting them to work for us?

Family Storytelling & Other Family Traditions

Every learning experience is attached to a story. It used to be that in most households, the time after dinner was devoted to sharing stories—perhaps lessons learned by the father and mother that day, as well as lessons passed down from their parents, their grandparents, and so on. Nowadays, that time is more often spent scooping our droopy-eyed children up off the floor where they have been sitting in front of the great American storyteller, the television, and hauling them off to bed. Could it be that we have delegated this time-honored tradition of transferring values, lessons and vital family stories to Hollywood? Is the art of capturing and sharing life's experiences becoming a lost art? This is an incredible loss, and it is having devastating consequences as our children are being molded by mindless television, music and advertising dollars.

Some friends of ours have created a tradition in their family that pulls life's daily lessons out from under the mattress. Each night they tell a story about the day starring their children and themselves. Their sons, Dan and Ron, become "Nad" and "Nor," and they go through the day's events while mom and dad mix in their day's experiences as well. For example, if the kids had gone to the pool that day, the story might be about what Nad and Nor did at the pool. Nad sees another boy drowning; what did Nad and Nor do then? Dad or Mom amplifies the story as it's being told to maximize the "lessons" learned. The stories move back and forth between fact and fiction, making the exchange both creative and educational.

Is there a similar tradition you could utilize in your home? The practice of sharing positive experiences or expressions of gratitude at the dinner table is a tradition that captures our experiences and gives them life.

When we looked at Core Assets, we were considering those abilities and gifts intrinsic to us, those capacities with which we were born, or to which we gravitate simply because of who we are. By contrast, Experience Assets are all of the experiences—both good and bad—that we develop over time: Education, skills, knowledge, techniques, systems, our reputation and even the networks of people with whom we establish bonds of mutual support. If the Core Assets are intrinsic to us, and part of our very nature, then Experience Assets are extrinsic—we acquire them over time. The best way to capture Experience Assets is to journal daily, or we will eventually lose them. We must deposit them in our family bank of life (See Chapter 11) to make them available for future withdrawal.

This is what Zolo was wisely doing when he shared his experience with us in his office at the Mongolian Stock Exchange. Zolo's experience now has a life of its own, and lives on—with or without Zolo—impacting thousands. This is capitalization, and this is legacy. The lessons of our experiences have value only to us until we share them with others; if they are not shared, they will never have value to anyone else.

Zolo's lesson came to mind when I was meeting with a client I'll call Larry, a highly successful, self-made businessman. Larry had just sold a very successful chain of retail stores. He was concerned that now that he had some time to spare, his kids resented him for having neglected them. I asked him the question I like to ask of all my successful clients: "What motivated you to become so successful?"

"We grew up poor," Larry said, "although, we kids never knew it. We never missed a meal, and we certainly never lacked for love in our home. My parents were fantastic, loving people, and my brothers and sisters and I enjoyed a great childhood.

"One night when I was about 10 or 11 years old, everything changed for me. There was a crawl space under the porch, and I loved to hide there with my dog. It was my favorite spot in the whole house; admittedly, it was not a very large house.

"I was in the crawl space when I heard my parents' voices above me. The tone in their voices was unlike anything I had ever heard before—it was one of abject fear.

"My mother was telling my father, 'We're almost out of money,' with an air of desperation in her voice. 'After next week, we won't have any money to feed the kids. What are we going to do?'

"I don't remember my father's response, but I do remember that he sounded just as terrified as my mother. This was an eye-opening moment for me, to say the least. My father had always been a rock, and my mother was a source of enormous strength as well. To hear them this terrified was far beyond anything I could possibly have imagined.

"Right then and there, I resolved that I would help solve this problem. I would go out and get a job myself, and contribute to the family earnings. And I would never, ever allow *my* family to find itself in the same predicament when I got older.

"Two weeks later, I got my first job, delivering newspapers. I've worked ever since. Eventually, I got a job sweeping out a corner grocery store. I ultimately bought that store and the rest is history. There hasn't been a day that I haven't been motivated by that experience under the porch."

"Do your kids and grandkids know about all this?" I asked.

He shook his head. "I never told them. I thought it would just be too embarrassing," Larry said.

This defining moment had never been shared! The failure to capitalize all of our assets—not just our Financial Assets—is a key reason why True Wealth fails to be transferred.

"How do you think your family sees you?" I asked. "How much of you do they really know if they don't know this story?"

"I think they see me as a workaholic," Larry said sadly. "I don't think they know me ... I don't think they really know me at all."

"What if you told them about that moment under the porch? You know, that moment under the porch was an asset to you. That one moment has motivated you every day of your life. You need to share it."

"Do you think they'd want to know about that? Would it do any good?" Larry asked skeptically.

"I'm not sure," I admitted, "but I think so. They would understand you in a completely new way. They might just recognize that all the time and hard work you put into taking care of them financially was to help them avoid that very moment in their own lives."

"I'll give it a try," he said.

He called a week later. He had told them the story of his under-the-porch moment. Decades of emotional distance evaporated in moments as his children and grandchildren suddenly understood fully, for the first time in their lives, who their dad was and why he had done what he had done, all for them. The family instantly drew closer as a result of Larry sharing his emotional turning point.

What exactly did Larry do? He took an Experience Asset and capitalized it—he shared it with others, and thus exponentially increased its value. If he had died without passing that story on to his descendants, the experience would have died with him, and they never would have known or truly understood him. Our Experience Assets are among our most valuable possessions, but they only reach their truest potential when we share them with the people to whom they will mean the most.

Today, what do you think is the favorite story that Larry's children now tell their children? Instead of feeling neglected because of their workaholic dad, Larry's children tell their children the under-the-porch story, and how Grandpa built a business that guaranteed financial stability not only for their family, but for hundreds of employees as well.

Capturing Experience Assets

I never knew my father all that well when I was growing up. He was a child of the Depression and worked hard his whole life. Even though I spent very little personal time with him, I learned from his example the value of hard work and integrity. I remember small moments that still resonate in me to this day. Once when I was still small, he swooped me up and said, "Hello, Hot Rod!" Man, when he gave me his full attention that way, I was on top of the world!

So, when I started thinking in terms of helping families make connections, deepen their bonds and share their values, I thought about the relationship between my father and me. I dug out my video camera and sat down with him. I wanted to ask him about his own childhood, and fortunately, he agreed to go along with whatever I had in mind. He told me about it in great detail, and for me, the most powerful moment on the recording was listening to him talk about his reaction to Pearl Harbor.

He and his brothers had been out hunting rabbits that Sunday afternoon in December, when they came home to hear the news about the bombardment of our westernmost naval base near Honolulu. He said that his older brothers immediately enlisted. He was too young to do so, but he yearned for the day when he could join up and serve his country as well. The memories my father shared with me on that videotape are priceless, and they represent an asset that my children and their children will possess for generations.

It was my children's turn in the spotlight after 9/11. I wanted to capture their reaction to those events, so that their children and grandchildren would be able to understand more deeply who they are, as well as *whose* they are. You can do the same thing with your family, and it doesn't take a cataclysm like a Pearl Harbor or a 9/11. Even if you don't have access to a video camera, you can capture their thoughts by recording them or simply by writing them down. It may seem like an insignificant step, but you are actually making a major shift: Instead of happenstance dictating what is transmitted to future generations, you are *choosing* what is remembered, what matters, and what will be available as a future Experience Asset. Family albums are great, but those photographs are mute testaments to bygone generations. Your family's stories will have greater impact than all the birthday snapshots and Disneyland montages put together.

Recently, I had the privilege of interviewing Hall of Fame basketball coach John Wooden about his "Experience Assets"—the events in his life that made him (in my opinion) into one of the greatest molders of character and talent our society has ever known. Wooden told stories of his childhood, memories of his parents and grandparents and a host of other stories that he had rarely talked about publicly. He shared his thoughts about his beloved wife of many years, Nellie, as well as his opinion on current topics such as education, religion, values and other inspiring thoughts and experiences. We created a video of this exchange as a gift to members of his family. We may also make it available to the public at some point with the proceeds dedicated to worthy charities supported by The John and Nellie Wooden Foundation. We captured Coach Wooden's wisdom and experiences and "banked" them for future withdrawal. You can't make a withdrawal until you have made the deposit.

The videographer on the project, Jim Ward, was so moved by the experience of observing John Wooden relate his past that he decided to do a videotape interview of his grandmother who was approximately the same age as Coach Wooden. He put it off for a couple of years. I would ask him about it, and he would reassure me that he did intend to get it done.

Finally, Jim called and asked if he could meet with me. He wanted to share a compilation of the interview with his grandmother. Together, we watched the interview.

"Grandma" was ninety-eight years young, vibrant, and laughing with a sparkle in her eyes as she recounted many of her life experiences. She counseled her children, grandchildren and great grandchildren. It was beautiful. I looked over at Jim and tears were streaming down his cheeks. He looked up at me and quietly announced that she had died in her sleep that very night. (Jim has since founded a company called One More Day Productions, which is devoted to capturing the life experiences of our loved ones.)

When many of us think about the past, we dwell on our errors instead of capitalizing our assets or experiences. We think about what we should have done, what we should have said, how we should have been, instead of focusing on what we experienced, what we learned and how we can share that learning with others.

At the beginning of this chapter, we asked a simple question: Who owns your past? By now, the answer is clear: You do. By recognizing the value of your experiences, by capitalizing those assets and sharing them with others, your life becomes your gift to the world. If we adhere to that principle, all of our experiences—good or bad—will increase the value of our Empowered Quadrant Bank, which we discuss in detail in Chapter 11.

What experiences have you had that have been defining moments in your life?

What experiences have you had that might benefit others and allow them to "stand on your shoulders," progressing further than they might have by knowing what *you* know?

How can you capture the experience of your family—parents, grandparents, siblings, aunts, uncles, etc.—and bank them for future withdrawals?

chapter 6

contribution assets

Until you integrate charitable giving from not just your financial quadrant, but from all of your quadrants, you will never be completely satisfied with your Financial Assets.

Want to leave a legacy? Here's one way: Write a check for $50 million to a nearby college and they will name a building in your honor. Easy, right?

Here's an easier—and less expensive—way to create a legacy: The next time you go to a drive-in restaurant, pay for the car behind you. Years ago when our son was recently married, he told us about an experience where the car in front of him at McDonalds had anonymously paid for his order. He was absolutely amazed. Since that time many of us in our family have continued this experience. In fact, it has evolved into a family tradition. About once a month, we, along with some of our children armed with a little of our savings, go out for what we call our "Legacy Breakfast".

Once seated, we scout around the restaurant looking for deserving candidates. Whispered comments like: "Look at that couple over there. They haven't said two words to each other. Let's buy their breakfast." Or "Wow! Look at all of those kids. I bet they would appreciate some help-let's buy their breakfast." We live close to an Air Force

Base and it is not unusual to see members of our Armed Forces and we sometimes will pay for theirs as well. Once we decide, we inform the waitress and then we make sure we leave before they are informed. We have yet to see the results of our anonymous giving ... a very fun and rewarding way for our family to leave a legacy.

What matters here is far more important than the meal you paid for. First, you're disproving the old saying, "There's no such thing as a free lunch." More to the point, you'll have gotten everyone around you thinking. In this case, "everyone around you" may include your kids, your spouse, the waitress or waiter, other restaurant employees (because you know the waitress or waiter will be telling the story to their coworkers), and, of course, the people whose meal you bought. You will have engaged each of them in an internal dialogue about "paying it forward," a way to repay seemingly undeserved good that appears in our lives. In other words, you don't have to die to leave a legacy. *You can do it right now!*

Spontaneous Legacy

When bad things happen in our lives, we often seek out someone or something to hold responsible. A classic example comes from Truman Capote's *In Cold Blood*, which told the true story of the murder of a Kansas farm family in the 1950s. When the murderer was brought to justice and asked why he had done it, he told of his own tragic past and said, "Somebody's got to pay for it." In this case, it was the innocent family whom he had slaughtered.

We all understand the concept of vengeance as an instinctive desire to repay evil, sometimes even taking justice into our own hands. We give much less thought to the question of how to repay *good* when it comes into our lives. Perhaps this is because so much good flows into our lives every day that we don't even notice it. We rarely think about the most valuable assets in our lives while we are enjoying them—our health, wealth, relationships, work, avocations and hobbies. As Joni Mitchell sang, "You don't know what you've got till it's gone." All too often, we don't appreciate what we have until we lose it.

The concept of creating a spontaneous legacy is a way to counter that all-too-human tendency to ignore the good in our lives. Whether you are buying lunch for a stranger or putting a quarter in someone else's parking meter, you are creating a conversation about how to appreciate what we have and how to share what we have with others. "Paying it forward" is a beautiful way to create a spontaneous legacy. By sharing the good with others, we change the thought patterns in the minds of others and get them to think about what's great in their lives and how they can pass along joy to more people.

When you do something for others you are, in essence, making contributions into your personal or family Contribution bank account. This is one of those magical accounts that continues to receive deposits, and no matter how many withdrawals are made, it never depletes the account. In fact, it does just the opposite. It is the ultimate viral marketing experience. Once it starts, it is difficult, if not impossible, to know where it might end. Like tossing a stone into a lake, the ripples extend outward, but you may never know where they end up.

I remember years ago listening to a story told by motivational speaker, Zig Ziglar. I have never seen the story in print and I have only heard it once, so I have to conclude that it has made an impact on me.

Mr. Big goes to lunch at the Country Club. He is late, as usual, and he huffs and puffs his way into the lounge to meet his clients. They have lunch mingled with intense business conversations and, of course, a few drinks. Unaware of the time that has passed, Mr. Big glances at his watch and sees that he is late for a very important two o'clock meeting at his office. He abruptly says his good-byes, rushes out to his big red Cadillac, and lays down two black patches of rubber as he races down the boulevard like an Indy driver.

Soon, the long arm of the law reaches out and stops Mr. Big. A ticket is his prize. Oh, Mr. Big is mad! He pulls up to the office, stomps inside and yells for his assistant: "Where is the file for my two o'clock appointment?"

The assistant is caught off-guard. Mr. Big can tell by the look on her face that she is not prepared. Oh, if Mr. Big was mad before—now he is livid! But as mad as Mr. Big is, his assistant is even more so. She is fuming! She storms into another office and screams at an unsuspecting secretary, blaming her for everything.

Oh, but if you think his *assistant* was mad—you should have seen the secretary. She could not get over it. She fussed and fumed the rest of the afternoon, and when she got home, her dog Fido happened to cross her path. And with all the fury of a hurricane, she gave that poor dog one swift kick!

Zig Ziglar concluded by saying: "Wouldn't it have been a lot simpler if Mr. Big would have just jumped into his car at the Country Club and headed directly to his secretary's home and just kicked the dog himself?

Seldom do we see the results of our actions. When I was twenty years old, I was in San Antonio, Chile doing missionary work. This was an interesting time in the political and social history of this South American country, and there was high anti-American sentiment at the time. There were no Americans that we knew of living in the area at the time, and no members of the religion we represented. This made for a very unwelcoming experience. My companions and I began to wonder how we could best serve these wonderful people who harbored such resentment toward us. We looked for opportunities to help, serve, or teach, but frequently found ourselves quite frustrated and wondering if we were doing any good at all.

We forged on. Ultimately, we met a man who had once lived in the United States and was the president of the local semi-pro basketball league. We were invited to play and we accepted. Through this experience, the attitude of the townspeople began to change, and, eventually, we actually became very well known throughout the city. Instead of throwing rocks and shouting insults, these people welcomed us into their homes with typical South American hospitality by saying, *"Mi casa es su casa."*

Eight months later, I was assigned to another city. As I boarded the bus, the crowd of well-wishers who gathered to offer thanks and wish me good luck was humbling. I said my good-byes, choking up as I waved *Adios*.

Recently, my wife Lori and I returned to San Antonio. The town hadn't changed much. It is an industrial port and the smell of fish brought back a flood of memories. We attended church in one of several beautiful chapels that now serve the members in this city. I had the opportunity to speak and share those first inaugural days of the church's existence in that area. Afterward, many came up and recounted experiences of learning from the early members whom we had met and were our friends. Several people suggested that I share my story with the church historian who lived in Santiago. He was originally from San Antonio, and many from the church knew him and offered to make the introduction. Unexpectedly and coincidentally, he appeared at the doorway of the church. He happened to be in town visiting family members, heard of our visit, and ran right over. He extended his arms and said in Spanish, "Mr. Lee Brower, I have waited over thirty-nine years to see you again! You don't know me, but I know you." To Lori, he spoke in English, "I even have a picture of your husband when he had hair!"

He was at the bus station the day I left San Antonio. Something that was said at the time motivated him to learn more about our religion. Four months later, he joined the church, becoming the first Chilean from San Antonio to go on a mission. I was blessed to see a ripple that began thirty-nine years earlier.

The concept of doing something for others is profound. In the Jewish tradition, the ultimate level of charity is called *Tzedakah* (pronounced like Neil "Sedaka"). *Tzedakah* is charity performed completely anonymously. If you want to elevate your personal esteem, or lift yourself out of the doldrums of depression, perform an anonymous, unexpected act of kindness for someone. You will immediately feel better.

The Family Contribution System

Many of us make charitable gifts, but we often do so in a reactive and decidedly unhappy way. Giving money to telephone solicitors who call on behalf of various causes, usually during the dinner hour, for instance. We have options: We can hang up on those calls, or we can say no. More often than not, we allow ourselves to be put down for twenty-five dollars or some other small contribution. How much of that money is actually going to the charitable cause for which it is ostensibly being raised? It's often hard to say. How many of those causes for which we are solicited actually match up with the societal issues that matter the most to us? Not too many. There is another way. Many families call it the Family Contribution System, and here is how it works.

If you examine the spending patterns of middle-class families, you'll most likely discover that most families not only contributed more money than they thought to charitable organizations, but they also missed a significant number of income tax deductions for those gifts. Why? Because most families lack systems for choosing the organizations to which they wish to donate, and they lack systems for recording just how much they've donated.

Most people live reactively, rather than proactively, when it comes to fundraising requests. They get requests from just about everybody for some charitable event or organization, and they end up pulling out their checkbook or their credit card, without really remembering why or how much. We tend not to remember how much money we gave for the local fundraiser for the high school, or a neighbor who collected at the door for some cause or another, and we even forget to include mileage to church or Boy Scout activities, which can sometimes be deductible. For these reasons, I want to share with you a technique for involving your family, so as to handle fundraising requests *proactively*.

You're sitting at dinner and the telephone rings. You answer the phone, and it's an individual identifying himself as a fundraiser for the Firemen's Association. While he's speaking, you can hear plenty of other people in the background, suggesting that he's calling from some very large call center (or even a boiler room), and he somehow doesn't really sound like a fireman at all!

Have you ever received a call like this? What were your emotions? Some people respond rudely; others just hang up, and some will simply acquiesce to the request. These responses are reactive rather than proactive. The Family Contributions System offers a very different, proactive way to respond. So let's run that scene again, but this time in a very different way.

You're still at dinner, and the telephone rings. You answer.

"Hi—I'm collecting for the Firemen's Fund. Will you make a contribution?"

You respond—proactively—and in a spirit of gratitude: "Thank you for thinking of us! We have a family organization that reviews all the charitable opportunities that are presented to us. We'd be very happy to evaluate yours. Would you be willing to send us an annual report so we as a family can evaluate it for next year's contribution budget?"

Suddenly, there's silence at the dinner table. All eyes are on you. They've never seen you respond to a call in that manner before. In fact, they've never seen anybody respond to a call like that before.

In the majority of cases the fundraiser is also caught off guard. Bear in mind, this is a sincere attempt to *proactively* take control of your Contribution Assets. Rather than simply reacting and not receiving a family benefit, you are able to take control of the situation, and if it fits with your passions and intentions, you may discover a cause that matches. Usually, the caller will either hang up, continue to attempt to persuade you to make a smaller bequest, or if the charity is set up for it, they may in fact send you the material you have requested. If they aren't set up to respond to your request, you can respond in the following manner:

"I understand," you respond calmly, still in proactive mode. "We're not set up to honor requests over the phone. I certainly wish you luck with your cause. Again, thank you for calling." Then, you may confidently hang up.

You are controlling the situation, not the caller, who is likely trying to induce feelings of guilt, and potentially inducing feelings of aggravation by calling during dinner and requesting money. It may take a moment or two, but your children will eventually shake off their stunned expressions and ask you what's going on. This is a great opportunity for you to talk about the difference between being proactive and reactive.

Discovering Your Family's Passions

Another experience you can share with your family is to discover their passions. At Quadrant Living, we call this conducting the "newspaper experience." Give every member of the family a newspaper and ask them to circle what they dislike with red, what they love with green, and what they find interesting in yellow. This helps you identify those causes that are of interest to each family member, or what current circumstances each member wants to support or prevent. Next, teach your family members how to read and evaluate annual reports from charities; in some cases, you may be learning with them. A wonderful resource for those of you who may not know where to start is the website www.charitynavigator.org. It will help you learn about the opportunities and pitfalls of charitable giving, what questions to ask and how to evaluate potential charities.

Wealthy families may establish family foundations. Families of moderate means may open a donor-advised account at a mutual fund company, which allows them to make contributions as money accrues and grows interest; you get income tax deductions for contributing to such a mutual fund. Yet any family can open a bank account dedicated to proactively hold and distribute contributions to their chosen charities.

You can create traditions in any manner that is meaningful to you and your family. The important thing is that everyone finds the experience meaningful, or at least is willing to keep an open mind about the value of the experience. The idea of turning unsolicited phone calls for donations into an example of a proactive response demonstrates that virtually any life experience, no matter how trivial, can become the focus of a tradition that transforms how a family thinks and operates. In this example of the Family Contribution System, you are modeling proactive behavior, as well as generosity, for your children, and *that* is an unbeatable combination.

This one exercise touches all four of the quadrants— Financial, because it has to do with the allocation of money; Core, because the newspaper exercise enhances the knowledge base of each family member as an individual and the family as a whole; Contribution, because you are making decisions about how best to contribute to society; and Experience, because you are creating a memory that will last as long as there are solicitors for charities, which means this tradition will last a very long time!

A huge advantage that emerges from the practices I've described in this chapter is that your children become much more aware of how the real world works. I'll give you an example from my own family. My daughter Natalie felt a strong calling to contribute to an organization that protected animals. Instead of the family instantaneously writing a check to one such organization, Natalie learned how to read the balance sheets and financial statements of that group. She discovered, to her dismay, that a shockingly small percentage of the money they raised actually went for the treatment of the animals, and that the organization kept for itself a very large percentage for salary, benefits and overhead. Natalie was stunned by the manner in which the funds were distributed, and she found other organizations that gave more of the money to animals ... and less to humans!

Another program that might be of interest is the humanitarian agency World Vision (www.worldvisiongifts.org). For small amounts of money, you can buy a goat for a man in a poor African country that will allow him to sustain his family. You can also pay for a sewing machine and lessons for a woman living in a Third World country to help her start a business and feed and clothe her family, or purchase a fishing kit for a hungry family. This is the kind of thing that all of us can do. It blesses the giver even more than the receiver to know one has changed the direction of another life.

My friend Doug Andrew, author of the "Missed Fortune" series of books, and a longtime Quadrant Living Advisor, tells of another approach to Contribution Assets and children. Doug was in charge of hosting an activity in his church for a group of young adults on a budget of $400. He invited a guest to their youth meeting who had a child being treated for a respiratory disease at Primary Children's Medical Center in Salt Lake City, Utah. She brought her baby, who could only breathe through a tracheotomy tube, and she told her story. After she spoke, they discussed the parable of the talents and handed each of the teens two dollars in an envelope—money that had been previously allocated for refreshments. The challenge was to see what could be done in six weeks from the $400 that was distributed (two dollars to each teenager). This project had to be accomplished amid their school activities and job responsibilities. The rule was they could not merely ask for donations; they had to perform acts of service and the two dollars were to be used as seed money.

One young man invested his two dollars in flyers to distribute to his neighbors, offering to seal their cement driveways to retard chipping and corrosion. He sealed six driveways within thirty days at sixty dollars each and netted a $240 profit.

Another young man also invested in flyers to offer to wire a spark-less wrench to their gas meter so they could shut it off safely in the event of an earthquake. He also strapped their water heaters to the wall or floor in order to make them earthquake safe. Several neighbors took him up on the offer, and he netted $180 for his two dollar investment.

Doug's two oldest daughters purchased gasoline and chain oil, borrowed a chain saw, and obtained permission to cut firewood from dead trees. They netted $160 each from the four dollar initial capital! Some young men and young women did such things as buying ingredients and selling dozens of pizzas. Others did lawn mowing and aerating. One young lady sold suckers where she worked at a fast-food restaurant.

All of the teenagers were excited to report their success six weeks later. Many told incredible stories and related the lessons they learned in the process. Remarkably, the average return on two dollars was a ten-fold increase! More than $4,000 was generated from $400 of seed money in six weeks!

The youth group next attended the Primary Children Medical Center's holiday fund-raising event, where they made the $4,000 contribution by purchasing several decorated Christmas trees donated to the event by others. They then delivered the trees to eight rest homes and sang Christmas carols and visited with the residents for a couple of hours. Several friends and priceless memories were made that day.

It just goes to show, it's not just about writing a check. It's about getting our children proactively involved in the decision-making process.

When most of us think about contributing, we wince as we reach for the checkbook. But charitable giving doesn't have to be that way. It can be a vehicle for creating a legacy as meaningful to the beneficiaries as it is to you and your family, and it can be a means of educating your children about the issues the world faces and involving them in the search for solutions.

The great visionary Buckminster Fuller used the term "planetary caretakership" to describe this approach. It's great to give $50 million to a university and know that your name is etched into granite forever. But a meaningful contribution doesn't require a seven-digit number. As even school kids have demonstrated, it doesn't require a check at all. The ways in which we and our children can contribute to society are limited only by our imaginations.

Lynne Twist suggests that: "When you let go of trying to get more of what you don't really need, it frees up oceans of energy to make a difference with what you have. When you make a difference with what you have, it expands." True Wealth shows up in the action of sharing and giving, allocating and distributing, nourishing and "watering" the projects, people, and purposes that we believe in and care about with the resources that flow through us.

No matter how much or how little money you have flowing through your life, when you direct it with a soulful purpose and passion, you feel wealthy. You feel alive and vibrant when you use your money in a way that *represents* you, not just as a response to tax planning, but also as an expression of who you are. You let your money move to things you care about. Your life lights up! That's really what money is for. We have the opportunity to direct our attention in the way we relate to money and when we do it, it empowers us. It becomes who we are and what we are about.

Contributors to society are those who are aware of their surroundings and sense the congruities and incongruities with their higher purpose. They know what activities violate their purpose and which promote their unified family purposes. It is a love of life brought on by a heightened sense of love for others and the environment, spawned by deep appreciation for those things that are harmonious and encouraging of their values. They see the trash alongside of the highway and they pick it up—just as they see other elements of society that need to be cleaned up. Yet, because their motivation is virtuous values-based, they do so in a loving and encouraging way. They are balanced within the quadrants, seeking optimization and growth of their assets, and they are lovingly willing to help and encourage family members and others. They know that if they focus on true asset optimization, all of the quadrants within the Family Empowered Quadrant Bank will be strengthened.

When a family is motivated from head to toe, generation to generation, the influence spreads like an ever-expanding web to connect every member of the family with each other and with everyone and everything on the planet. The resultant gift to society and to each other is confidence. The interdependence of contribution-based families, united in purpose, fed by the certainty of knowing their intentions and actions are harmonious with their collective vision, leads to a continuous, unselfish, non-self-promoting impact on society which in turn feeds ever more appreciation and confidence.

What social causes do you feel strongly about? (For example, animal rights, resource conservation, education, world hunger.)

What organizations work with the causes you support? (Perhaps you'll need to do some research here; some organizations may be readily apparent, but others may not be as well known.)

Has your family created a written philosophy statement to serve as a guide for future philanthropic contributions?

chapter7

financial assets

"All progress begins by telling the truth."
Dan Sullivan

Financial empowerment is possible for everyone—no matter what your past or current experience of wealth or poverty. It begins when you wholly accept your current financial situation and commit to following the rules laid out in this chapter.

Accepting your current situation means you will no longer waste precious time and energy on self-pity, self-doubt, resentment, envy or frustration. Rather, you will begin to search for the vehicle that will get you where you want to go with an open mind, compassion and focused commitment, making a determined effort to follow the rules of financial empowerment.

In Chapter 12, The Five Phases of Wealth, we identify the stages of what we call "financial wealth ownership." Each stage has the potential for either the development or loss of wealth. Even though I outline five phases, most of our readers fall into one of three categories of wealth:

> *one.* You are a Striver, earnestly searching for that vehicle that you can drive. You know there is more for

you and you are anxious to succeed. You keep searching. You have marvelous intent and someday you will find your vehicle.

two. You are a Driver. You believe you have found the vehicle for you. You may even be driving several vehicles at once. You have an idea of where you are going; however, you have difficulty actually describing it. You feel overwhelmed and unable to focus on your most efficient vehicle. You are a good driver, but you can't stand taking care of all of the details.

three. You are an Arriver. You have earned, acquired, created or inherited sufficient Financial Assets that by most estimates you will not outlive. You may struggle with your own form of guilt. Why me? Why am I blessed with this financial abundance? You recognize that others have been deeply enriched through your investments, businesses and philanthropy. Yet, you still search for that true sense of fulfillment and meaning. You also worry that your children and grandchildren may be negatively influenced by your affluence. Will your life's work be in vain or will there be a lasting empowering legacy?

Most of us hope to become "Thrivers." Thrivers are those who have found the perfect vehicle to drive and know how to replicate the process. You can take away a Thriver's worldly possessions and he or she will in short time reacquire the same level of financial wealth. True Thrivers not only know how to do it for themselves, but also leave behind a legacy of followers who continue to build from where they left off. They are always creating and always contributing—dynamically, unselfishly and purposefully.

How do we become the best we are capable of becoming, leaving behind a legacy of heirs who reach even greater heights of achievement? Whether you are financially rich or just starting out, the rules for financial empowerment remain the same.

Rule 1: Know Where You Are

All progress begins by telling the truth of where you are now. If you intend to build the bridge that will transport your family's wealth into future generations, you must begin from where you are—not where you want to be. The fruits of the experiences that brought you to where you are now will become the foundation for building your generational bridge.

Rule 2: Know Where You Are Going

A clear vision of where you are going is essential. It must be specific. You must be able to see, feel and experience the destination. Once you have the vision, you can establish and prioritize the appropriate steps to get you there. In the following chapter, we will take you through the Clarity Experience, which will give you a clear indication of where you desire to be. The vision that you create through this experience is your current horizon. Where is your horizon located? It exists *only in your mind.* As you move toward your perceived destination, you will discover that your horizon keeps moving. It moves as you do, and no matter how hard you try, you will never reach that horizon. This is good; otherwise, life would get terribly boring.

Rule 3: Do the Essential First

In today's environment it is not uncommon to focus our efforts on very important issues at the expense of the essential. For example, I know an individual who devoted his life to working with those living in famine only to lament later in life that he had lost his family in the process. A more common example may be the simple act of wanting right now what may be considered a luxury and sacrificing valuable savings that would have gone toward retirement to acquire it. Experience has shown that by identifying and systematizing our true intentions (the essential) you can achieve the peace and joy that comes with arriving at your desired destination.

Instead of thinking of your Financial Assets as a whole, I invite you to place them into four "money buckets": Contribution, Stability, Independence and Get Rich. We call this the Quadrant Bucket Theory. Let's take a look at the purpose of each money bucket and see how it will help you create a new vision of building and safeguarding your Financial Assets and those of your family.

The first money bucket is the Contribution Bucket (see figure 7-1). I recommend you take at least ten percent of each month's income and commit it to philanthropic causes. You're probably thinking, "If I'm already living on 120 percent of my income, how can I possibly give ten percent to charity?" In his book *Wealth Without Risk*, Charles Givens suggests that if your spending is already at a 120 percent of your income, you won't even notice the next ten percent that bumps it up to 130 percent!

You may ask, "Why would I put money into charity before paying my bills and taking care of other obligations?" My experience has been that by giving back you reinforce your attitude of gratitude. You better equip yourself to

7/1

Contribution Bucket: Giving Means Having More

Contribution

-Give 10% of your income to philanthropic causes
-Include your core and experience assets as part
of your charitable giving.
-Appreciating what you have starts with giving back

make good decisions and may find yourself less impulsive. This is not a new concept. Malachi, an Old Testament prophet, taught: "Bring ye all the tithes into the storehouse, that there may be meat in mine house, and prove me now herewith, saith the Lord of hosts, if I will not open you the windows of heaven, and pour you out a blessing, that there shall not be room enough to receive it. (Malachi 3:10)

Charitable giving is an evidence of gratitude. Gratitude is in and of itself the great attractant. Gratitude affects our thoughts. Thoughts with action create results. Grateful individuals attract great relationships and great opportunities. Think about it. Do you enjoy being around grateful people? What about those who walk around spewing of ingratitude? Do they attract you? Ungrateful people always feel they never get what they deserve. You may ask yourself: "Am I a grateful person or an ungrateful person? How do others know that I walk with gratitude?"

Until you integrate charitable giving from not just your financial quadrant, but from *all* of your quadrants, you will never be completely satisfied with your Financial Assets. You will always want more, bigger and better. Addiction can be defined as never having enough of that which we don't need. Can you become addicted to these things—more cars, bigger houses, more clothes and more money? If you desire to avoid or overcome this addiction, focus on your Contribution Bucket first. By focusing on service to others, interacting with those who have needs greater than yours, we begin to nourish an ever-increasing attitude of gratitude.

Most of us spend money unconsciously. We don't really keep track of where it goes, and we end up wasting a lot of money on things that don't really matter to us. You may have seen the bumper sticker that says, "I spend money I don't have, on things I don't want, to impress people I don't even like." We're all guilty of this to some extent or other. When we become conscious and aware of how much money we are spending, and what we are spending it on, a lot of our unnecessary spending melts away. Suddenly, there is more money to take care of our responsibilities, and it becomes easier to provide financial security for our families, and to have enough to contribute to society. If you're wondering where the money to fund this new contribution practice is going to come from, look to Deepak Chopra, who said, "The money will come from ... wherever it is right now!"

What happens when we take the first ten percent of our income and place it in the Contribution Bucket? This attitude of sharing provides a sense of confidence and self-worth that is essential to growth. When we donate money to the charitable, educational, environmental or spiritual causes that we believe make a difference, we are demonstrating to ourselves—and to the universe, if you like—that we truly feel we have enough. We only share when we are convinced that we can get by without the piece that we give up. Donating that first tenth of our income— *activating* the Contribution Bucket—helps us develop the self-confidence that allows us to say, "I believe in my ability to make not just enough money to pay the bills, but also enough to be supportive of the needs of others—even the needs of individuals I've never met." This optimistic stance creates a mindset of affluence and prosperity.

In Chapter 11, The Empowered Quadrant Bank, I'll share with you new ways to involve your family in proactively making charitable donations. For now, it's enough to recognize that we live in an abundant world, and that when our hand is open to give, it's most open to receive. By committing to place ten percent of our income into our Contribution Bucket, we are entering into that sense of flow so vital for the creation and maintenance of True Wealth. Giving is having more.

Our second bucket is the Stability Bucket (see figure 7-2), which begins with an investment in you. The idea is to pay yourself immediately after you have allocated to the Contribution Bucket and before you pay anyone else.

7/2

Stability Bucket: Make an Investment in Yourself

-Pay yourself first because in today's world
saving = freedom
-Establish a spending plan and stick to it
-As your savings grow, add other things that will
protect your family such as insurance, wills,
and trusts

This creates a level of financial stability and security for yourself and your family. The concept of paying yourself ahead of your other obligations is not a new one—you can find it in many books on personal finance. The concept is so important because most of us pay ourselves last, if at all. We are so caught up in paying bills, making minimum payments on our credit cards and keeping one step ahead of the creditors that we fail to focus on the importance of saving. The problem with paying ourselves last, after all the bills have been handled, is that it practically ensures that a family will never save anything. Take a look at the extremely low savings rate in our society and you'll see that "pay yourself last" means that few people are building financial stability.

Savings in the world today is freedom. When we don't have savings we limit our choices. When we are economically fit we have the ability to choose. When we lack savings, or worse yet are saddled with debt, our freedom to take advantage of opportunity is limited. If you value freedom, it is *essential* you choose to invest in your contribution bucket and then increase your stability by creating savings for yourself.

I'd like to take it a step further. Establish a spending plan and agree to abide by it. Within that plan, set aside an amount of money where it can grow safely and conservatively. This is your rainy day fund. Determine an amount that is comfortable to you. It can either be a percentage of income or a fixed amount. Then, resolve that that money is sacred and only to be accessed in a true emergency.

In addition to your savings, focus on putting assets into the Stability Bucket that will protect your family. As it accumulates, use some of the money in your Stability Bucket to purchase insurance and appropriate legal documents, such as a will or trust. If you are on a limited fixed income, your first policies will probably be term insurance. Get the most coverage you can afford. It guarantees a benefit for your family if something happens to you and it can also lock in your insurability. Often when you need insurance the most, you are unable to get it at a good price—if you can get it at all—because of health issues that may make you uninsurable. There are a number of services that will shop for the cheapest rates for you with financially stable insurance companies.

If you have a growing estate, you should consider an investment grade life insurance policy that can maximize the benefit to you. Properly structured within your Empowered Quadrant Bank, life insurance can provide a benefit that is free from both income and estate taxation. I know of no other financial vehicle that has the ability to provide a tax-free death benefit while accumulating cash reserves on a completely tax-deferred (or, in some cases, tax-free) basis.

You may ask, "How can I start saving money when I don't even have enough to pay my bills?" Please go to my website, leebrower.com, and click on "Free Reports". Select the document, "101 Ways to Increase Savings Now!" Many families have seen immediate results after implementing some of the common sense ideas from this booklet.

Security comes from knowing that your family is taken care of in the event of emergency. Pay yourself first, but be sure to spend some of that money on the appropriate forms of protection for you and those you love.

Once we have a handle on our Contribution and Stability buckets, we have a newfound peace: We are meeting our own needs and sharing our abundance with those around us. It's now time to activate the third money bucket, the Independence Bucket (see figure 7-3). Independence focuses on our standard of living. Are you adequately creating a secure retirement for yourself? The money we place in the Independence Bucket will find its way into the investments you need to create financial independence and maintain your quality of life. True freedom begins when you have earnings that, combined with savings,

7/3

Independence Bucket: The Second Best Time is Right Now

Contrib

Stabi

Independence

-Add low-risk investments such as real estate, mutual funds, and retirement plans, that will secure your financial future and quality of life exceed your spending needs. This discretionary income should then be prudently and strategically managed for low risk returns.

There are various tax-advantaged plans that will actually accelerate your retirement accumulations. Often times employers will offer profit sharing or similar plans where they will actually match a percentage of your contributions. Don't miss this opportunity to optimize your retirement. If you are self-employed, you may wish to consider the tax benefits of a defined benefit retirement plan. In certain instances, a defined benefit plan can accelerate the amount you can deduct from taxes into your retirement plan. This is especially useful if you are older and wish to catch up. Don't underestimate the power of tax-deferred savings. This book will not delve into the various kinds of qualified plans, mutual funds, and other forms of investing. (Go to www.quadrantliving.com for a list of certified Quadrant Living Architects; they can help create the perfect plan for you.) The point I wish to share is that by *committing* to financial independence—by committing money to your Independence Bucket—you are doing more than creating financial stability, which is the role of the second money bucket. Instead, you are building for your financial future, and this can be an exciting and even exhilarating achievement for people who have never tried it.

When do you start placing money into your Independence Bucket? Everyone I've ever met wishes they had started years earlier. But as the Chinese adage goes, "The best time to plant a tree is twenty-five years ago. The second best time to plant a tree is right now."

The Independence Bucket is meant to create a safety net for the future. Many people confuse the Independence Bucket with the fourth bucket, the Get Rich Bucket. I hope you won't make that mistake! The Get Rich Bucket is the place where we hold the financial investments that carry a higher degree of risk for reward and loss. It's essential to fund our Independence and Get Rich buckets, but it's also essential to remember that these are two very different buckets.

I can't tell you how many times I have met with families that have wonderful incomes and their Get Rich Bucket is overflowing. They have diamond mines in Brazil, high-risk equity deals, penny stocks and so on. Sadly, they often don't have much in their Contribution, Stability and Independence buckets. If fact, frequently those buckets are nearly empty.

Many people make the mistake of taking the money that they need to invest in financial *independence* and "bet the ranch" on high-risk schemes. It rarely works.

7/4

Get Rich Bucket: But Slow & Steady Wins the Race

Contri
Stabi
Indepe
Get
Rich

-Add high-risk investments only after you have a handle on the first three buckets.

We differentiate between an Independence Bucket and a Get Rich Bucket to emphasize that when it comes to developing wealth, *slow and steady wins the race.* All of us know more people who grew wealthy through steady investment in secure real estate and conservative equities than by playing the stock market or investing in Peruvian copper mines. When you begin to distinguish between your Independence Bucket and your Get Rich Bucket, it's harder to make big—and potentially disastrous—bets on uncertain propositions.

There's a place in your portfolio for high-risk investments that offer the possibility of high returns, and you may well get rich from those investments. But no one should take a chance with the funds that they need for financial security. Understand that your Get Rich Bucket is to build your family bank for future generations. This is your family empowerment bucket. Properly configured, regardless of how much financial wealth you accumulate, this wealth can continue to serve your family and society for generations to come.

The concept of money buckets—Contribution, Stability, Independence and Get Rich—works remarkably well for families at practically every point on the socioeconomic scale. As you get a handle on each bucket, you earn the right to put more into subsequent buckets. When an opportunity presents itself, ask yourself, "Which bucket does this belong in?" Your answer will dictate whether or not you should even consider the investment. The only real mistake you can make is to decide that you can't afford to divide your money in this fashion. Take it from someone who's been working with affluent families for decades and who has a pretty clear idea of how those families achieve their wealth: You can't afford not to!

Rule 4: Don't Go It Alone

Even if you are savvy when it comes to finances, engage the services of someone who is unbiased, who will hold you accountable and who has a successful history of assisting families grow toward their vision. Get educated; talk to people and friends you trust. Find out who they work with. Evaluate your own advisors. Do they have a bias toward a particular specialty or commodity? Do they truly represent you or will the fact that they are pressured to sell a product or bill a certain minimum amount of hours subconsciously influence their advice?

Be proactive in selecting who you choose to work with. You have to be precise on what you expect from them. Check their references and validate their experience. They must know your vision of the future and have the experience and networks to assist you in getting there.

Look to your networks and relationships. Having an advisor who works within a community of other advisors who perhaps have different specialties, but understand and complement each other, is a distinct advantage. Also, being a member of a community of other families whose financial status is similar to yours and who are willing to share their experiences is invaluable.

Rule 5: Adjust Your Course Frequently

Just like a ship at sea, you must trim the sails to adjust for current conditions and keep yourself on course. A good advisor will have a system for frequent updates on current conditions, changes and other important updates. Planning is not an event. It is an ongoing process. I can't tell you how many times I have heard individuals say, "Oh, I have done my estate planning." Estate planning is a process, not an event. I refuse to call it estate planning. To me it is "Family and Estate Leadership." If you did your estate planning yesterday, it is out of date today.

The reason this quadrant is known as the Financial Quadrant is because it is the first quadrant we talk about when we begin the Napkin Presentation. It provides stable datum. When I ask the question, "What do you think of when you hear the word assets?" most people respond with money, real estate, stocks, etc. As the quadrants begin to work in your life, you will soon come to learn that the Financial Quadrant is really about security, asset protection and dynamic value creation. If you follow the Quadrant Bucket Theory, and then focus on creating value for the planet, allowing the laws of attraction to work for you, you will always be rewarded—and most times financially. The world always rewards value creation.

What Financial Assets do you have in your Contribution Bucket? What is the monitory value of those assets?

What Financial Assets do you have in your Stability Bucket? What is the monitory value of those assets?

What Financial Assets do you have in your Independence Bucket? What is the monitory value of those assets?

What Financial Assets do you have in your Get Rich Bucket? What is the monitory value of those assets?

partthree

the practice of quadrant living

chapter 8

creating clarity

"Hurry seeks ever to make energy a substitute for a clearly defined plan. The result is as hopeless as trying to transform a hobby horse into a real steed by brisk riding."
William George Jordan,
The Majesty of Calmness

As you get older, does time speed up or slow down? Is it just me, or does Christmas arrive sooner each year? It seems like just yesterday, I was cradling my children in my arms, and now I watch as they cradle my grandchildren. Yes, each year does go by faster and faster. But does it have to? I have a theory, and it has to do with hats.

Have you ever exclaimed that you were "wearing too many hats"? Do you remember your first "hat"? What was it? As we move into adulthood, do the number of hats we are wearing increase or decrease? Let's make a list of some of the hats we might be wearing:

Father, mother, son, daughter, sibling, aunt, uncle, grand-parent, protector, provider, investor, taxpayer, worker, employer, employee, teacher, mentor, spectator, coach, cheerleader, go-fer, chauffeur, student, golfer, philanthro-pist, cook, maid, gardener, arbitrator, vacation planner, leader, manager, church member, speaker, motivator, voter, nurse, lover, exerciser, homeowner, landlord, etc.

Could it be that the more hats you have, the faster time goes? Can you remember as a youngster anxiously awaiting the arrival of your grandparents to show up in forty-five minutes so they could take you to the zoo? As you stared at the clock, did time go by slowly or quickly?

Forty-five minutes does not seem like a long time for most of us, but when we were staring at the clock, those forty-five minutes seemed like an eternity. At that moment, how many hats were you wearing? Only *one*—a youngster waiting to experience the zoo. Your only thought was "How much longer till they get here?"

Have you ever been in a serious car accident? Did time speed up or slow down? I remember a stormy winter night in eastern Oregon many years ago. The driving was treacherous. I was steering my Volkswagen bus over a high mountain pass. My son Nathan, then six months old, was sleeping peacefully in a small travel bassinet behind the front seats. Suddenly, we began to slide helplessly on a sheet of invisible black ice. As we slid onto the gravel shoulder of the road, the van caught immediate traction and began to teeter precariously. As the vehicle rolled over, I instinctively reached my hand to the back seat and held little Nate in place. Life, as I knew it, suddenly went into slow motion. My senses were on high alert and I was keenly aware of the one hat I was wearing. My only role at that moment was to protect my family. Miraculously, no one in the van was seriously hurt. It was one of the most frightening moments of my life.

As anyone who has been in a serious accident can tell you, it feels as if time slows down as the accident unfolds. It was probably mere seconds from the time our vehicle began to lose its traction until it came to rest, but it seemed like minutes. I saved time to do the most important thing I could do. The question is: Why did time *seem* to slow down in that experience?

I believe the answer has to do with the number of hats we are wearing at any given moment. During the accident, I was wearing one hat—father seeking to protect his son. One hat plus one focus equals a sense of time standing still. The more our attention is diffused by the different roles we are playing at a given moment (the number of hats we are wearing), the faster time seems to pass. The child waiting for his grandparents is also wearing only one hat. Time, therefore, hangs endlessly for him.

The Cowboy Hat

An example from popular culture that illustrates the varying degrees of time is country musician Clint Black. For Black, as for most highly successful performers, there were years of working his way up to the big time. Once stardom is conferred upon an artist, everything changes. He is no longer wearing one hat, that of "musician trying to make it." Instead, he is wearing a multitude of hats: superstar musician; CEO of a corporation; investor; overseer of recording studio and touring dates; manager of attorneys, accountants, and other professionals charged with handling business affairs; and so on. The shift in Clint Black's lifestyle and concept of time are reflected in two songs that he wrote, one before stardom hit, and the second after he became a household word in country music.

The first song was called "Killing Time," as in, "This killing time is killing me." One hat. The second song was called "No Time to Kill." As Clint Black's responsibilities sped up and the number of hats he wore increased, his perception of time sped up. The same thing is true whether we are a student in Albert Einstein's lecture hall, a country music superstar, a business owner or a homemaker. The more hats we wear, the faster time speeds along.

One of my buddies used to say, "The sooner I fall behind, the more time I have to catch up." It's a funny expression, but it has serious meaning. The sooner we fall behind, the sooner we are thrust into a reactive mindset. We aren't making things happen—instead, things are happening to us, and we are doing our best to keep up with the onslaught of tasks and responsibilities that get dumped on us. "Reactive" living is neither comfortable nor especially productive. So the question is this: How do we move toward a proactive approach to life, so that we feel in control of our time, our emotions and our lives?

The answer is to focus on the number of hats we are wearing at any given time. The more hats we wear, the more our focus becomes divided; thus, the more it feels as though time is slipping away. Not too many of us are "killing time" these days; we're all way too busy. Do you feel like you are bouncing off that imaginary (but nonetheless challenging) ceiling of complexity? Do you feel overwhelmed by all of the hats you are wearing? By the time we get home at the end of the day, we wonder where the time went. And that's what we find ourselves asking at the end of any significant benchmark in our lives. Life today conspires to spread our attention so thin that we feel frustrated and exhausted instead of happy and exhilarated.

If we're going to take control of our time and slow it down, we need to reduce the number of hats we wear, or at the very least, be aware of the amount of time we devote to the wearing of each hat, and find a way to prioritize our hats, so that we don't get caught in a maze of endless to-do lists without ever accomplishing our heart's true desires.

In short, we are looking for clarity. When we focus on what's *essential*, instead of merely important, our lives advance in meaningful ways. There are many "important" activities to which we commit ourselves. Is it important to be on the board of a worthwhile charity? Is it important to have dinner with a key business contact? Is it important to work out at the gym? Absolutely! But when measured against our *essentials*, we have to ask ourselves, "At what cost?" We probably can't afford the time to do everything we would like to, but by focusing on the essential first, it is possible that a lot of the things that are important will still get done. My experience is that you *will* get more done— the essential as well as the important.

In high school, I played football, held down a part-time job, was a student body officer, and attended a church seminary class every morning at 6 a.m. I received my highest grade point averages at this time. I had to do what I felt was essential first—my high school and religious studies. By focusing on the essential first, I was able to accomplish much more. Imagine measuring time by your accomplishments, rather than in minutes, hours, months, and years. Instead of repeating the remorseful declaration of time flown by, you can sit back and proudly proclaim, "Wow, this is awesome! Can you believe everything that we accomplished in the last year? I can't believe we did all this. So much was accomplished in the short span of just twelve months."

Do you want to reap more in less time? Would you like to achieve more with less effort? Clarity will help you discern the important from the essential.

I predict that if you consciously go through the Brower Quadrant Clarity Experience that follows, you will discover an elegant system for achieving more—faster and more easily. You will come out of it with your own personal vision statement, which will allow you to clearly see the future *you*.

All you need is a pencil, a few sheets of paper and an open mind.

The Brower Quadrant Clarity Experience

Step One: Take a look at each of the four domains of the Brower Quadrant: Core, Experience, Contribution and

Financial Assets. To help familiarize yourself with all of these important assets, list all of the aspects of your life that relate to each of the four areas. You can make these lists on a separate piece of paper *or here in the book*

Core Assets (family, health, spirituality, happiness, ethics, values, unique ability, relationships, and heritage)

1.
2.
3.
4.
5.

Experience Assets (wisdom, formal education, life's experiences—good and bad, systems, ideas, traditions, alliances, skills, talents, and heritage)

1.
2.
3.
4.
5.

Contribution Assets (taxes, private foundations, charitable contributions of Financial Assets, as well as
contributions of Core and Experience Assets)

1.
2.
3.
4.
5.

Financial Assets (cash, stocks and bonds, retirement
plan, businesses, real estate, and other material
possessions)

1.
2.
3.
4.
5.

Step Two: One of the great questions that Dan Sullivan
(co-founder of Strategic Coach) introduced me to years
ago is the "R" Factor Question™. This has become such
a cornerstone link to other concepts taught by Strategic
Coach that he has even trademarked this question:

Imagine sitting here three years from today looking back to today. What has to have happened for you to feel pleased with your progress both personally and professionally?

For our purposes, we refer to this as the Three Year Vision Question. This is a vitally important question. Three years, I believe, is the perfect timeframe for this sort of planning. When we start thinking about expectations that are five to ten years out, the end date seems so distant that we tend to procrastinate or even despair. Three years seems to work well for creating a meaningful and achievable vision.

By contrast, when we set deadlines for ourselves that are short-term, we may not be giving ourselves enough time to make truly meaningful shifts in our lives. (You'll note that I don't use the word "goals." More about that later.)

Before we begin, let's outline three agreements on how to optimize this experience:

> *one.* We begin each expectation with "I am ..." or "We are ...," answering as though the intention has already occurred.

> *two.* We want to "drill down" to get specific. For example, if you were to write, "I am physically fit,"

ask yourself, "What does 'physically fit' mean to me?" You may respond with something like: low blood pressure and cholesterol. Then, continue to "drill deeper": This time you might put your actual target blood pressure and cholesterol levels. Continue to do this with each response until you have the most specific answer you can find. The more specific you are the more meaningful this experience will be.

three. Most people have several objectives that fall within each of the four quadrants. Make sure you have at least one intention, if not more, in each quadrant. As you begin to answer the Three Year Vision Question, think in terms of the quadrants. Bear in mind that we're not talking about creating aspirations for the rest of our lives; we're talking about a specific measurable amount of time and asking ourselves what milestones we would like to pass to feel a sense of accomplishment and pride in each of the four quadrants.

Everyone's aspirations are different, but we're not talking about everyone. We're talking about *you*. Just let it flow. List everything that comes to mind. It is important that you don't hold back or make any judgments at this time. If the thought hits you, write it down. Be specific. Don't just say, "I want to be rich," for example, or "I want to be out of debt." For the best results, describe what being out of debt *means* to you. What does it look like? What does it feel like? Drill as deep as you can. For example, you might write, "I have eliminated my mortgage and all consumer debt and have $100,000 liquid in the bank," or "I have sold my business for $100,000,000." *That* is more specific.

Do Not Restrict Your Vision

Do not restrict your vision to financial achievements only. Make sure your list includes several items for each region of the Brower Quadrant. How do you see your family? How would you describe the relationship between you and your spouse? Describe your health, your values, and those of your children. Include your spirituality or belief system, your unique abilities and God-given talents.

What experiences do you see yourself capturing over the next three years? Will you travel? Where? How often? What new skills will you learn? Will your networks and alliances expand? What about your reputation and that of your family and/or business? Will you continue to augment your education?

What about your charitable contributions? Have you identified those causes that you wish to support (with money, time, contacts or strategies)? Where do you want to make a difference—in your church, community, neighborhood, state or country? What about disease prevention, education, abuse, global warming, hunger or other areas of concern? Where can you and your family have impact? Will all of your family be involved? Will your family discover the passion for giving?

Now, make your list.

Once you have listed everything you can think of for each quadrant, it's important that you share this list with someone. If you have no one with whom you feel comfortable sharing it, read your list out loud. In fact, it's a good idea to read the list out loud several times.

Note how you feel. Do you feel good? Are you beginning to experience a sense of ownership for these future achievements? I hope so.

Next, imagine that I have a magic wand and I am going to wave it over your head, and as I do, everything you wrote down will not come to pass. I repeat: *will not* come to pass!

If you said you were going to be out of debt, you will have more debt. If you said you would be in perfect health, you will be sick. If you said you were going to travel, you stayed home. If you said you were going to involve your family in feeding the poor, you did nothing.

How does this make you feel? Upset, mad, sad, unbelieving?

What if I were to say that, out of the kindness of my heart, you could take one, and only one, achievement or experience back? Which one would you choose? Look at your full list and *pick only one.*

Perhaps it is to be completely out of debt or to sell your business. Perhaps it is for you and your family to have perfect health. Possibly, it's to have an incredible relationship with your spouse and children or grandchildren. It could be that you want to be more spiritually in tune, or that you have a cause bigger than yourself to channel your time, energy, influence and money. *Pick the one achievement or ambition that you believe is the absolute most essential for you.*

I know it's tough to pick just one, but for the sake of this exercise, you must do it. When I went through this exercise, I struggled to come up with only one. As I thought it about it, I concluded that the greatest achievement I could have would be to be completely aligned with God's vision and purpose for me. I could have chosen perfect health or a phenomenal relationship with my wife, Lori. Or any number of other items listed. In any event, you will decide which one is the main catalyst for you. There is no right or wrong answer.

With this one ambition fully secure, do you feel any better? Say it out loud: "I am ..." or "We are ...". Then, complete the sentence with your one achievement. Do you *own* it?

Now that you have selected the most essential achievement, identify the quadrant it most belongs to. Sometimes it will actually overlap two or more of the quadrants. But pick the one quadrant you believe it most closely coincides with.

Write your first choice in the appropriate quadrant on the following page or on a separate sheet of paper. When finished, you will pick one achievement for each of the other three quadrants not represented by your first choice. Insert each of those achievements in the quadrant it belongs to. For example, if your first choice is a Core Asset achievement, write it in the center quadrant. It can be in any one of the four quadrants. There is no right or wrong choice.

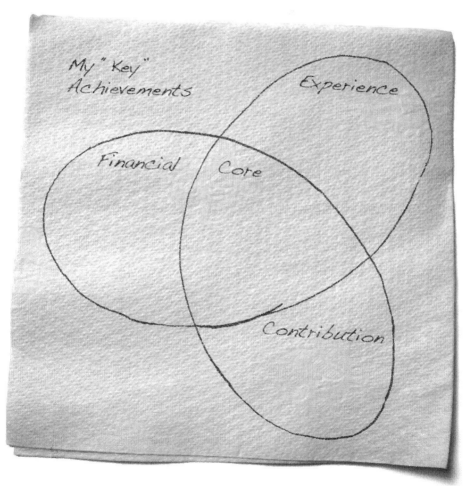

figure 8-1

Choose an achievement for each of the other three quadrants and write them in the appropriate space on the previous page.

Share your four most important achievements with someone else; or at least read them out loud. Think. Write. Share. Own. When you think, write and share them—they are yours. You *own* them!

The next step is critical. Place the quadrant with your four most important achievements alongside your brainstorming list, which includes everything you wrote down to start this exercise. Review the lists carefully.

Consider looking back to today three years from now and you have achieved the four things listed in your quadrant. Ask yourself, "What is the likelihood that most of the other things I identified in my first list would be accomplished, too?

Do you think it's possible that if you achieved your primary financial desire that most, if not all, of your other financial ambitions would follow? If your objective was to eradicate credit card debt, and you completely focused on that, wouldn't your net worth rise? Would you develop habits that would help you in other areas of your financial vision? Better credit and reduced debt may make it easier for homeownership. What if you chose to focus on preparing to sell your business? What would happen to the value of the business? What effect would the sale of the business have on other financial achievements?

Let's look at the Core Assets region of the Brower Quadrant. Sometimes people say that if they could improve only one thing in this area, they would develop a deeper, more meaningful relationship with God. If, every day, you made sure that you lived your life in harmony with what God envisioned for you, isn't it entirely possible that most everything else in your life would improve as well?

Recently, I was doing this exercise with a large group of young people and one woman approached and asked if she could have "two" focus achievements in the Core area. She said they were both equally important. I asked her if she would share them with me.

She said she chose perfect health as her Core three-year achievement target. But equally important, she wanted to meet the man of her dreams. My recommendation was to go with her first impulse. Perhaps the universe was trying to tell her something. It just might be that by focusing on the Core Asset target she was inspired to write first, she will have increased self-esteem and confidence and will attract that man of her dreams.

Now, let's turn to Experience Assets. Some people might want to focus on their education, either by finishing an incomplete degree or by finally tackling that Master's program. Let's use this as an example. If you were to complete a degree, what would that do to the other Experience Assets? You will now have more knowledge, more skills and more options to advance in your current or desired career. As your education level rises, typically so does your income. Additionally, your network of great contacts and relationships will expand. By paying attention to these new relationships, you will experience results in other areas of your listed ambitions. So there is a spill-over effect from the Experience region of the Brower Quadrant into the Financial and into other quadrants as well. Other examples might include capturing your family history, recording stories from parents and grand-parents, writing in your personal journal, traveling and developing new networks or new traditions. The more you do, the more you're capable of doing. By focusing on one element within the Experience Assets region of the Brower Quadrant, you gain clarity and create a situation where many, if not all, of your other dreams and aspirations become a reality.

Finally, let's turn to Contribution Assets. As we have seen, Contribution Assets are ways in which we contribute to society—either involuntarily, by paying taxes, or voluntarily, out of our sense of gratitude, by volunteering our time, experience, and wisdom to the organizations and causes that mean the most to us. Let's say you get involved with a community outreach project, such as Habitat for Humanity, and in three years want to have made a significant difference by having built four homes in your community. The expression "doing well by doing good" often comes into play in such a case because when we involve ourselves with community activities, we meet other like-minded people with whom we may develop business relationships, friendships or even romantic interests. At the very least, we increase overall happiness purely because we've made a contribution.

"A rising tide lifts all boats" is another relevant expression, and in this case, the rising tide is clarity, and the lifted boats are the results we attain within each of the quadrants by focusing on just one key.

Step Three: Now that you have completed Step Two, you have your "Four Keys," or Clarifying Visions. When you have clarity about your primary desires within each of the four regions of the Brower Quadrant, the wobble in your life vanishes. You have set the course to turn your life into a finely tuned vehicle, operating on four perfectly balanced tires.

When you have done this, the most important qualities in the world are yours:

You have *velocity*—the ability to get more done in less time—because you're wearing fewer hats.

You have *focus,* because you know exactly what you want to accomplish, and you now focus on those activities that will generate the greatest results.

You have *energy,* because you no longer have that desperate feeling that comes from being tied down to your lengthy and expanding to-do list.

And you have *confidence,* because instead of trying to attain dozens of sub-goals, you have your life focused on your Four (specific) Keys and four is an extremely manageable number of dominant desires for one person to achieve.

Now, take out a fresh piece of paper. You've got the perfect vehicle for you—it's perfectly tuned and in balance. Now you need the perfect track on which to travel. You are going to create your Quadrant Vision Statement. This is critical. This will give you a vision of what you are capable of. This will propel you into the future. As you read this each day, you will do what you need to do to attract all of the great relationships and opportunities necessary to make your vision a reality.

Are you ready? Are you willing to take the time to do this? I predict that if you take the time to carefully ponder this next question, write the answer, share it with someone immediately, and then review it daily, you will elevate to heights you never thought possible!

Here is the question: If we were to meet three years from this very day, and you have (of course) achieved each of your key achievements, or Four Keys, and all of the attendant ambitions that you have envisioned for yourself have also been realized, *who are you now and what are you now capable of?*

Respond by beginning the paragraph with "I am ..." A few actual samples of what others have written follow:

"I am a spiritual giant who enjoys using many gifts of the spirit. I am led by God in all my decisions and conversations. I am highly respected in my home, work and community for my kindness, wisdom, perspective and excellent listening skills. I have a highly successful and functioning company, which produces $1 million plus per year, blessing my family, staff and clients' lives. I am very healthy and vibrant, filled with joy and gratitude. I control my time and thoughts. I bless the lives of many through my church service and my family foundation. I am now capable of accomplishing whatever I choose to do under the inspiration from God and counsel from my wife."

"I am a devoted and respected wife and mother. I am a leader, not a manager. I am guided by my highest spiritual values. I am capable of capturing my growth, knowledge and experiences for both my family and future generations. I have a broad world view and experience that frees me from small mindedness and self-centeredness. I am present and a good listener. I am a good communicator and I help elevate the lives of others. I am financially secure for both today and the future."

"I am grateful to our Lord for everything I am and will be. I am a vibrant, healthy and blessed wife, mother and daughter. My life is joyful, peaceful and abundant. I am a positive role-model for my daughter, with the ability to demonstrate solid family leadership. I am an educated, respected and trusted businesswoman with strong relationships in my network. I am a passionate contributor in my community with my time, ideas and monetary support. I am financially secure. I am a best-selling author. I am a mentor. I am physically fit. I am balanced in my professional and personal responsibilities. I love and am loved deeply. I am capable of achieving anything."

Congratulations! You now have a new way to look at your life! You will still have multiple hats to wear, of course, but you now know which four hats are most essential to you. Write your Quadrant Vision Statement on a 3"x5" card, or put it in your planner—somewhere you can carry it with you and read it throughout the day. As you begin each new day, ask yourself this question: "Just for today, what steps can I take that will move me towards my key (Clarifying Vision) in each quadrant?"

Thoughtfully consider the steps (no matter how small) that—*just for today*—you will take.

Do this, and you will be amazed at how much you will achieve in all areas of your life. You truly will be the "I am ..." you describe in your Quadrant Vision Statement. You will attract the relationships and opportunities that will guarantee that three years from now, you have reached your milestones, and probably checked off a few other items on life's to-do list as well. You're no longer spreading yourself too thin. You're no longer living *reactively*. You have knocked off a few hats, and you are driving your vehicle on that proactive Road to Predictable Results! I expect you will experience an amazing surge in productive richness and self-esteem.

Exercise:

Think about all the different hats you wear. There's your spouse hat, your parent hat, your work hat, your member of the community hat, your homeowner hat, your investor hat, your taxpayer hat, your coach hat, your go-fer hat, your boss hat, your teammate hat, your friend hat, your listener hat, your protector hat, your teacher hat, your student hat, your board member hat, your sibling hat, your provider hat, your bail-your-kids-out-of-trouble hat, your chauffeur hat, your maid hat, your bill-paying hat, your dispute resolution hat, your church hat, your cook hat, your laundry hat, your get-in-shape hat, your keep-yourself-healthy hat, your disciplinarian hat, your vacation and travel hat, and so on. How many more hats can you think of?

chapter 9

gratitude rocks

"Happiness consists not of having, but of being; not of possessing, but of enjoying"
William George Jordan,
The Majesty of Calmness

In the last ninety days, have you had a positive experience? Would you be willing to write it down and then share it with someone? Would you be willing to do that right now?

In 1995, I attended my first Strategic Coach® workshop with Dan Sullivan in Chicago. Strategic Coach® is a company that utilizes proprietary concepts and systems to aid business owners in their quest to break out of the ceiling of complexity and bring more balance into their personal and business lives. Dan asked us to write down five positive achievements from the previous ninety days. Little did I know the incredible impact this seemingly trivial exercise would have on my life. He called it a "Positive Focus."

I now begin each day, each meeting with staff and clients, and each family meal with a Positive Focus. When we share our positive experiences, they acquire a life of their own and live on without us as others learn from it and also share it. An experience never shared will die with us.

I spend a couple of days each month coaching successful entrepreneurs for Strategic Coach®, an experience I have enjoyed for almost ten years. Like Dan, I begin each day-long workshop by asking each participant to list five achievements, personal or professional, that have been attained in the last ninety days.

The first time we do this the silence is typically so complete that one might think they had stumbled into a monastery. These individuals, among the most successful of business people in our society, are hard-pressed to come up with five positive events that have happened in their personal or professional lives. I'm not sure I know why. I assume it's because they are moving at such a fast pace, they don't take time to celebrate their daily achievements. They have no system for noting what is positive, meaningful and therefore worth remembering. As a result, the positive events of their daily lives slip away, noticed at the moment, but rarely *captured*, because the person has moved on to the next event, the next dilemma to be resolved.

I begin every meeting in this way for two reasons. First, physicists tell us that it's impossible for darkness and light to occupy the same space at the same time. I believe that the same thing is true when it comes to negativity and creativity. In my opinion, creativity and negativity cannot dwell together at the same time—at least, not for very long. We may not even be aware of what negative experiences or thoughts we bring to a meeting. By taking a few minutes to capture positive experiences, we move into an attitude of gratitude. Mood-enhancing chemicals created by our own bodies are actually released into our systems as we focus on positive thoughts. Usually, people who participate in this exercise have an immediate boost of energy and creativity.

Second, I believe that *capitalizing* our experiences is very important. To do this, we must first capture the experience, and then release it, so it has a life of its own. We capture it by writing it down and sharing it. First we think it; then, we record it; then, when possible, we share it. This is called "banking the experience"—depositing it in the Quadrant Bank for future access.

In my workshops, I often spend as much as an hour devoted solely to the Positive Focus exercise—it's that important. It usually takes a while for these business leaders to get the hang of the process, but with a little bit of time and deep concentration, they eventually come up with some great experiences. My classes aren't filled with negative people. It's just that life often goes by so quickly, and they have no system in place for recording the positive events that happen.

Before long, these participants become very proactive. They know that we are going to do a Positive Focus every time we meet, so they start taking note of their personal and professional experiences as they happen. Soon, they are struggling to limit their list to *only* five achievements. The importance of recalling and capturing these events cannot be underestimated. By doing so, individuals shift their focus from a state of negativity, in which the only thing that matters is the next cloud of dust on the horizon, to an awareness of the successful businesses and lives they have created for themselves and those around them—or even more meaningful, the joy that comes with personal or family experiences. Even entrepreneurs making lofty incomes need a little prodding when it comes to concentrating on what's great about their lives.

Two such moments stand out in my mind. The first was a business owner who had completely forgotten about the birth of his first grandchild. He became a grandfather, but in the rush of events, he had not remembered the event as one of his top five. He was obviously extremely proud and delighted about becoming a grandpa! But like so many of us, he was moving at such a pace that single events, regardless of their importance, were often buried in the inner chambers of the brain, suppressed by other recent events and the struggle to handle today's pressing schedule.

The second was another highly successful entrepreneur who sat stumped while everyone else was writing down his or her positive experiences of the previous ninety days. Later, as others were sharing their lists, he suddenly remembered: He had given a gift of $150,000 to his church, which had flown him and his wife to Dallas to an annual assembly to honor them for a lifetime of generosity and philanthropy. It was one of the greatest moments of his life, but it had slipped his mind.

Why? Remember, look first to the system. Let's not blame ourselves. I believe we all have so much going on in our lives that when we finally take the time to capture our positive experiences and blessings, we struggle with remembering significant events. These individuals, as accomplished as they could be, simply lacked systems for capturing the abundance in their lives. They scurry, as do so many of us, within a cycle from activity to crisis without having a method for capturing, sharing with others and celebrating the life achievements and milestones that mean so much. Million-dollar moments were slipping away because there were no systems in place to capture them and bank them for future withdrawal.

In the financial world, appreciation typically means that you have an increase in the value of your investments. For something to increase in value in our day-to-day world, it must first be appreciated. By acknowledging gratitude for someone we are increasing the value of that relationship. In today's "get it done" world, it becomes very difficult to remember the daily experiences, opportunities and relationships that we appreciate and value. So, how can we add more gratitude and appreciation into our lives?

W. Edwards Deming, an American professor and statistician widely credited with improving production following World War II, taught that whenever there is a breakdown, it is invariably due to the lack of a system. I have learned that most failures are a result of the system—not the individual. Conversely, it would be safe to assume that most successes are also a result of the system.

What systems do you have in place to increase gratitude in your life? Capturing and sharing your Positive Focus is one system for accomplishing this. Remember, to increase the value of something, it must first be appreciated. If you desire to add more meaning to your life, begin by capturing and appreciating all of the wonderful experiences and relationships in your life—regularly and systematically.

Positive Parenting

Can the concept of Positive Focus be applied to families? Positive Focus is absolutely one of the most powerful tools that we have as parents. I believe in it so much that I would never give it up. Initially, a certain amount of commitment is necessary on the part of parents seeking to implement this system.

This is where leadership comes in. Leaders are consistent. Lead by example, and it's best not to push your family too hard too quickly. Give them time to adapt to the idea until they adopt it for themselves. Let's see how this might work in a household that includes a teenager. As many of us know, getting information out of a teenager is only slightly more difficult than getting information out of a prisoner of war. It's comical—unless *you're* the one dealing with the teenager. We all know the drill:

"Where'd you go?"

"Nowhere."

"What'd you do?"

"Nothing."

It makes you wonder whether all teenagers belong to a secret army that has conditioned them to share with parents and other interrogators only their names, ranks, and serial numbers.

Teenagers have compelling reasons not to share with parents or other authority figures where they've been or what they've been up to. This is true even when they've been doing something perfectly moral and acceptable. Adolescents want to live their lives away from the prying eyes of their parents for many reasons, not least of which is to begin the process of breaking away to establish their own lives. As any parent of teenagers will tell you, this often is an excruciating process for all involved. The challenge is to find ways to convey your values to a sullen, uncommunicative (but otherwise terrific) teenager.

So, what's a parent to do? When you first try to employ Positive Focus at the dinner table, you may run up against that stonewall of resistance that parents know all too well. When you ask your teenager for some piece of good news, the reaction is likely to be wordless, just a shrug followed by a slurp of soup. You've got to hang in with this one! You can't force a teenager to accept the idea of Positive Focus as a regular dinner table event, but you *can* lead them gradually to the concept.

Day 1

Parent: "Anything good happen at school today?"
Teenager: "You kidding me?"

Day 2

Parent: "Anything good happen at school today?"
Teenager: "How long are you going to keep this charade up?"

Day 3

Parent: "Anything good happen at school today?"
Teenager: "Well, nothing bad happened today!"

This is a start! In fact it's actually a great start. I refer to this as a positive negative. Be consistent and predictable. If you commit to using Positive Focus, don't turn away at the first sign of potential disharmony. Sometimes you might think: "Whoa, this is turning into a very uncomfortable stand-off. I want him to say something positive and he refuses." It may even go further downhill: you might be tempted to say "What's wrong with you? Are you trying to tell me that nothing positive happens in your life?"

"That's exactly what I am telling you!" is the likely answer.

What happened to that positive moment? Be careful that you don't slip into that unpredictable territory of reacting.

Maintain the proactive role of leading from gratitude and respect.

May I share a few hints that I have learned after years of doing this at work and at home? In either situation, begin your request with these four very powerful words: "Would you be willing ...?"

Rather than announce that you will be doing this new thing, just make the simple request, "Would you be willing to share a positive experience from today or something you are grateful for?" If you still encounter someone who refuses to participate, I recommend that you take the person aside, put your arm around him or her, and say something like this: "This Positive Focus thing is something that I believe in. I would love to establish a tradition of regularly focusing on a few of our positive experiences. I know sometimes they are difficult to recall. Would you be willing to support me in this—even if you can't think of a positive experience? It would mean a lot to me if you shared anything that you are grateful for. Can I count on you to support me with this?"

In our family, we even taken it one step further. When any of us arrive home, whether it is from school or work, we must share three positive experiences before we can complain about something. At times this is tough, but I give credit to my wife for making us stick to it. Usually, by the time we share three positive events, we have forgotten the negative experience. We also apply this rule to school friends and guests who come to dinner.

If you are consistent long enough, you will eventually transform your conversations, and with it, the culture in your family or workplace. Positive Focus is indeed an acquired taste for the young (and perhaps for most of us). But once everyone gets used to it, it's hard to go back to the way things were. Before long, those around you will not only be reporting the great events of the day, they will be actively seeking them out. At home, you will have trained your children to consciously watch for positive moments and outcomes, to capture them in their memory, and to share them with you. Soon, you'll find that kids are competing to see who can go first, sharing their positive moments. They will have begun to focus on what's working in their lives and not just on the typical disasters that make the teenage years so excruciating (for both teens and their parents!). You move them out of the reactive Valley of Hope and Despair and onto the highway of proactive Predictable Results.

Positive Focus provides a system for capturing the happy events in our lives that might otherwise go unremembered. Whatever we turn our attention to grows, be it a positive or negative. Positive Focus has an amazing ability to shift completely the point of view of any human being. It offers an alternative to the traditionally negative thinking that so many of us lapse into unconsciously. More important, Positive Focus allows us to bridge the gap between us and those we seek to influence, at home and at work.

It is not unusual for captured experiences to actually evolve into family traditions that survive through the fourth generation and beyond—carrying with them a valuable Experience Asset to many generations of a family. Traditions are a great way to institute a system that will outlive you.

The following is a real world example of Positive Focus in action: Recently, my good friend and Canadian partner, Jay Paterson, called me, excited to share a Positive Focus.

"Lee, can I share my Positive Focus with you? This morning I shook the hand of my grandson! He weighed seven pounds, four ounces and his grandpa was the first human to shake his hand."

I was honored that he would call to share this experience with me. I congratulated him and then asked the clarifying questions that lead to truly capitalizing this

Experience Asset. Remember, we must first capture it; then give it away or share it, which he did. So now, how does he *capitalize* his experience?

"Jay, what a marvelous experience! Why was this meaningful to you?"

This may seem like a silly question, but if you answer "why," the value of the experience is elevated automatically. (Try this experiment at the end of this chapter.)

Jay explained that it brought home the miracle of life, it deepened the love and respect he had for his daughter and his wife, and that he was filled with the love that only a grandfather can have for his grandson.

"Now that you have captured this experience, what further progress can you make to assure it is *capitalized*, or has a life of its own?" I asked.

"Wow! That's a tough one." He thought about it for quite awhile and came up with a great idea. "I will begin a tradition of shaking my grandson's hand every year on his birthday to strengthen our bond and remind him that I was the first person on earth to shake his hand."

Now for the final question, the one that puts everything into motion: "What can you do today to insure that this tradition will continue?" In other words, what is the first step that can be taken?

"There is no guarantee that I will be here next year," Jay said, "so my first step will be to write down my feelings about this experience and my vision to see this as a tradition that is handed down from generation to generation. That way it will be recorded, and hopefully, he will carry on the tradition."

The Gratitude Rock

Systems don't have to be complex to be effective. In fact, they can be surprisingly simple. What if you could create a system for capturing the abundance inherent in your life just by bending down and picking up a small rock?

There have been times in my life when I was so focused on the overwhelming tasks of each day that I moved further and further from an attitude of abundance. I found it hard to see the good in practically anything. I was in a fog, over-focused on the future, ignoring the learning experiences of the past, and flying through the present like an F-16 after the *Star Spangled Banner* at the Super Bowl. It took the struggles of one of my daughters to awaken me from this self-centered sleep.

Several years ago, my daughter was struggling with some heavy personal issues. She finally hit a major breaking point and was ready for some help. Together, we researched and selected a program that we both felt would have a positive impact on her life.

At the door of this facility, we hugged and said our good-byes. With great emotion, my daughter hung her head, and through smothered sobs, uttered words of regret. She apologized for being a burden on our family. My heart ached.

I put my hands on her shoulders and looked into her beautiful tear-filled green eyes. "Sweetheart, by going through this experience, will you come out the other end better off or worse off?"

She lifted her chin slightly and proclaimed that she would be much better.

"And if you allow me and the rest of our family to go through this experience with you, and we learn from this, are *we* going to be better off or worse off for having gone through this experience?"

"Better," she said hesitantly.

"So, let's get going! I am ready if you are."

Before we parted, I left her with one last thought. From the age of twelve, she has had the nickname of "Mariposa," which is Spanish for butterfly. I reminded her that she has known the struggle of the caterpillar, the loneliness of the cocoon—and now she was about to experience the elegance and the strength of the butterfly.

Later that same day, I took a solo trip to a California coastal resort to get away for a few days, for some introspection and to write. The next morning I walked on the beach, contemplating life's challenges and opportunities. As I strolled slowly along the edge of the foam, breathing in the fresh morning breeze that tumbled off the waves, my gaze was drawn to a dark-colored rock. It actually seemed to be glowing and I couldn't resist picking it up. I turned it over, and there in black was a clear image of a butterfly in flight!

My heart stopped. My throat tightened. Was this a message to me to focus on the beauty of the flight?

I knew it was meant for my daughter. When she received this little rock in the mail (sent priority FedEx), she was

anxious to call me and find out what this was all about. I told her to keep it close to her, and to think of something that she was grateful for every time she touched it. I told her I was going to hunt for my own rock and I would do the same.

Every morning when I get dressed and reach for my wallet, there sits my rock. It immediately reminds me to drop to my knees and express gratitude for the many incredible relationships, experiences and blessings in my life. I actually visualize those things for which I am grateful. I conclude by visualizing the day ahead and the outcomes I desire as I place the rock in my pocket. I am reminded of my vision and gratitude each time I touch the rock throughout the day. Then, at the end of the day, after I place the rock on my bed stand, I capture the experiences of the day (writing them down), and once again take time to express my appreciation.

Wherever I go, I now collect rocks. I give them to anyone who is looking for a simple system to keep them in an attitude of gratitude. Sincere gratitude is the magnetism that allows the law of attraction to work. I remember once hearing "Gratitude may not be the greatest of virtues, but it is the parent of all the others," and I couldn't agree more.

Once, an audience member approached me after a speaking engagement and asked, "Lee, have you ever lost your swing?"

I needed clarity. If he was talking about golf, I was not sure I had yet found my swing.

He continued, "My relationship with my family is horrible. Work sucks, my kids are causing us grief, and I have lost my zest for just about everything. I just don't know what I'm going to do. Life's just unbearable."

"Here," I said, reaching into my pocket. "Take my rock."

The man's eyebrows shot up. A rock? Clearly, this was the last thing he expected. He eyed the rock in my outstretched hand with suspicion.

"What do you mean?"

"Here, take my rock," I said again.

He took it from me, and I shared the story of how I had found my first rock, and what all the subsequent rocks had meant to me.

Ninety days later, he came back and returned my rock.

"What's this for?" I asked.

"I'm giving it back to you. I found my own. And I've probably given away a dozen or so to others."

We shared a laugh.

"It's made all the difference in the world. The meaning of that rock has completely changed my life," he added.

A few nights later, a friend from South Africa was visiting me in Salt Lake City. He accompanied me to a rehearsal by the Mormon Tabernacle Choir. I was getting my car keys from my pocket, and he noticed the rock. "What's that? Why are you carrying a rock?" my friend asked.

I explained it to him, and we went to listen to the choir. He became very emotional as they prepared a program in honor of our military forces. Those in the audience who were in the Air Force stood up with the choir and sang the Air Force hymn. Next, those from the Coast Guard stood and sang the Coast Guard's song, followed by attendees associated with the Army, and so on. It was a very emotional experience for all who were there, but especially for my friend from South Africa.

"You know, things are different in my country," he said. "We fear the military. We have absolutely no fond feelings for them." He had gotten caught up in the emotion of seeing a nation and its military united in purpose.

As we left the hall, he turned to me. "Where is that gratitude rock?"

I had never officially called it a "gratitude rock" before. I handed it to him, and to my surprise, he rubbed it for a moment before handing it back to me. He then reached into his wallet, took out a twenty-dollar bill, and gave it to a homeless person nearby.

"There but for the grace of God go I," he said.

About two months later, he sent me an e-mail: "I have a son with a rare form of hepatitis C. I don't know if he's going to live. Could you please send me three Gratitude Rocks?"

He was affording me more spiritual authority than I possessed (especially considering I plucked my rocks from some rather inauspicious locales!). But I couldn't turn down a request like that, so I found three Gratitude Rocks and sent them to him immediately.

I didn't hear from him for six months. Then, a second e-mail arrived: "Thank you so much. My son is better. He had a complete, one hundred percent recovery. I've now sold about a thousand of these Gratitude Rocks for ten dollars each. All of the proceeds go to hepatitis C research. Thank you again."

I don't attribute the power of healing to a rock. However, I do believe a positive, grateful attitude is a major contributor to the healing process.

After reading the e-mail, I sat for a moment in shock. I thought of the one thousand South Africans walking around with Gratitude Rocks in their pockets, and how these glorified stones reminded them each day of how grateful they were to be alive, of the beautiful events that had taken place that day—events they might not otherwise have noticed or remembered.

On top of that, thousands of dollars had been raised for charity! It all stemmed from one person bending down to pick up a small rock at the beach. It's hard to remain cynical in the face of such developments.

Recently, I was asked by Rhonda Byrne, the creative force behind the incredibly successful movie and book, *The Secret*, what I considered to be the "secret" to success and happiness. I responded with gratitude and commenced to share the story of my South African friend. That story was dramatized in *The Secret* and consequently, millions of people have been exposed to the power of gratitude and the system of the Gratitude Rock. Every week I get numerous e-mails from around the world expressing gratitude and sharing stories of how the rock in their pocket has made an impact on them or someone they love.

After speaking at an event in Los Angeles, I was approached by a gentleman who shared that exactly one year prior, he had lost his wife to an illness. He recounted that he was bitter at life and at God. How could this happen to him? His wife would never get to experience the joy of grandchildren, the freedom of retirement nor the intimacy of growing old together. Then, someone shared *The Secret* with him. He reached into his pocket and pulled out a small stone. "After reading *The Secret*, I realized I was not living in gratitude. I was a 'victim'. That moment I chose to be a 'victor'! I went out to my wife's garden and carefully selected this rock. It has been with me since.

Every time I touch it I think of the great blessing she was in my life, how I am a better person because of her, all of the wonderful experiences and trials. I honor her and our memories with the way I live each day!"

So what is a rock in your pocket? It's a system and *systems don't have to be complex to be effective.*

A rock is a system that attracts abundance into our lives. It's a system for reminding us to focus on gratitude, to appreciate all that is good and great in our lives, to think of the people we love and cherish, and to remember the wonderful things—great and small—that happen to us each day. It reminds me to reflect on those individuals and experiences I cherish when I arise in the morning, and at night before I retire. It is a system for capturing moments that otherwise go unacknowledged and unshared. The assets we fail to capture, we lose—as do the generations that follow us. And, as we know, our most important assets are not the financial ones.

On a lazy summer day, a child tosses a pebble in a pond and watches the rippling circles travel to shore, touching and reshaping everything along the way. So it is in life. Our daily actions are the social equivalent of a pebble tossed into a pond; the ramifications of our actions— positive or negative—influence people, even those at a great distance. If a mere pebble can displace hundreds of gallons of water, what might be the ripple effect of a fist-sized rock?

Just for today, every day, I choose to be in an attitude of gratitude. I get to choose how each day begins, and receive the positive energy that accompanies my awareness and gratitude for all the many blessings in my life. You get to choose, too.

List ten things for which you are grateful:

1.
2.
3.
4.
5.
6.
7.
8.
9.
10.

This gratitude list can get you started on using the Positive Focus concept in your home. Where else might you employ this practice (i.e., at work or in other organizations in which you participate)?

Think of a positive experience you have had recently. To "capture it," write it down. Now, ask yourself *why* that experience was positive, and write your response below:

chapter 10

goodbye goals

"You can have anything you want if you want it badly enough. You can be anything you want to be, do anything you set out to accomplish, if you hold to that desire with singleness of purpose."
Abraham Lincoln

The word "goal" has been banished from my vocabulary. In fact, in our office, we have agreed to a two-dollar penalty for anyone who uses the word!

Have you ever set a goal? Have you ever set a goal and not achieved it? Have you ever set the same goal again, and again not achieved it?

When you frequently, or even occasionally, set goals that go unachieved, what happens to your self-talk? Are you saying supportive things to yourself, or do you begin to "dis" yourself? When your brain is engaged in negative self-talk, do you know what chemicals are emitted into your system? What are you attracting? Could you actually be attracting more of the very thing that blocks the attainment of your intentions? (Notice I did not use the "g" word.)

Many years ago, I read about a study conducted at Yale University. It has appeared in several books and I have also heard noted motivational speakers refer to it regarding the power of goal setting. According to legend, in 1953 researchers surveyed Yale's graduating seniors to determine how many had specific, written goals for their future. The answer was three percent. Forty years later, researchers polled the surviving members of the Class of 1953 and found that the three percent with written goals had accumulated more personal financial wealth than the other ninety-seven percent of the class combined!

That's great for the three percent, but if this study is accurate, there must be something we can do for the other ninety-seven percent. How do we help *them* achieve? Curious, I started to personally research this report. I discovered that the business magazine *Fast Company* and their researchers had already completed a very thorough investigation of the study. They had asked a prominent motivator for the source of this study, which had been referred to in one of his books. They were referred to another author/speaker who said that he had gotten it from a different motivator, who referred the researchers from *Fast Company* back to their original source. They finally decided to go to Yale for information, but nowhere in Yale's records did they find mention of such a study. They contacted many from the class of '53, eventually discovering the study never took place! It never happened. The assortment of consultants, trainers and motivational speakers who put the power of setting personal goals above all else have been spreading this story for years—many in good faith, I'm sure.

Am I saying that goal-setting is wrong? Actually, I like goals, when they are used correctly. What I object to is the common misuse, misunderstanding and misapplication of goals. The traditional principle of goal-setting needs to be revisited. I strongly believe that the improper use of goals can be dangerous.

Traditional Goal Setting

What happens when you, or perhaps your employees, set a goal (or, as is often the case, goals have been set for them), and two-thirds of the way through the targeted time period, they conclude that the goal is unattainable? Do their efforts increase or decrease?

What happens when you fall short of your desired goal? Do you focus on the fact that you didn't attain your goal, or do you celebrate what progress you did achieve? Most people focus on the first.

I believe that if it were possible to fully understand the negative impact of the improper use of goals on individuals, families, businesses and society in general, we would be astounded. When we set goals *without a vision*, or have goals thrust upon us, the negative psychological effects of failing or falling short can be devastating. Many individuals move from feeling guilty to feeling shame. Guilt is feeling bad about *what* we have or have not done. Shame is feeling bad about *who* we are. Guilt, in and of itself, can be a helpful emotion as long as we learn from it and let it go. Shame, on the other hand, can be incapacitating. When our self-talk moves from the positive to the negative, we have to guard against moving into shame.

Let's say you have set a weight-loss goal for yourself, and you have accomplished about fifty percent of your goal; you dropped eleven of the twenty-two pounds you intended to lose, and your loss has hit a plateau. Where is your focus? Are you celebrating the positive experience of losing those eleven pounds, or are you feeding your potential "failure" with thoughts of what you did not accomplish? If you're like most people, you already feel that you haven't lived up to your own expectations. You begin to focus on what you did not achieve, which begins to *attract* the very results you dread, and the lost weight reappears.

Many of us are familiar with Napoleon Hill's dictum, which lies at the heart of the entire personal growth movement: "Anything the mind can conceive and believe, it can achieve." Armed with enthusiasm, we feverishly start writing down goals, especially around

New Year's Day. More often than not, we set expectations for ourselves that—because of our process of goal management—become unattainable. When we focus on time frames, every unmet deadline can work against us, eventually leading to paralysis and the decision to "start over." The cycle continues. We fail to congratulate ourselves for the positive steps we take, and soon we have set ourselves up for more failure; and we do it again and again and again—perhaps nearly every time we set goals for ourselves! Goals are not wrong; the way most people *use* goals is wrong.

Think of a goal as the little boost you need to get into motion. When you learned to ride a bike, you may have stood holding the bike, making occasional attempts, until Dad came along and gave you a little shove. Then, you were in motion, and you just took off. You may want to use goals to get you started, but a clear vision is what will keep you going until you reach your destination.

The Pringle Theory

I have been blessed to share quite a few special moments with former UCLA basketball coach John Wooden. The John Wooden-coached UCLA teams scaled unprecedented heights that future sports organizations are unlikely to match. Under his masterful guidance, the

Bruins set all-time records with four perfect 30-0 seasons, eighty-eight consecutive victories, thirty-eight straight NCAA tournament victories, twenty PAC 10 championships, and ten national championships, including seven in a row.

Those who know Coach Wooden best say he is a gifted teacher. I believe he would say that teaching is his passion. Now in his late nineties, Coach Wooden still visits elementary schools, challenging young students to be the best they can be and training them in good sportsmanship. From my perspective, Coach Wooden is someone who walks his talk; he is an inspiration to many. He often shares his Seven Point Creed, given to him by his father when he graduated from elementary school, with all who will listen. Number four of the Creed is "Drink deeply from good books, especially the Bible." (You can see all seven of Coach Wooden's Creed at www.leebrower.com.)

I decided that if the great John Wooden reads from the scriptures daily, I would do exactly the same! I decided to read at least one chapter every night. It wasn't that I hadn't attempted this before. In fact, I had attempted this many times, but at some point I would begin missing a day or two. Soon, frustration and discouragement would set in. When I skipped a night, I would tell myself that the following day I planned to read two chapters of scripture. I was determined not to fall behind on my new spiritual quest, and I was certain that I was not going to allow my "goal" to slip away from me. Something would inevitably come up the following day, however, causing me to miss a second night! I would then vow, of course, to read three chapters the following day. Before long, I was so far behind on my "goal" of a chapter a night that I felt worse about my spiritual assets than I ever had before I set the goal! My self-talk would become negative, focused on my failings. I blamed myself for not accomplishing my goal. My focus was on perfection instead of progress. And we all know that perfect is found in only one place—in the dictionary between *perestroika* and *perfecta*.

I was learning to look to the system for solutions, rather than lay blame. Yet I continually blamed myself or other circumstances whenever I fell even slightly short of any goal.

I asked myself if I *owned* the goal. Or was this a goal imposed on me, or perhaps something I was pressured to establish? Do our children set goals that they desire to achieve or that their parents want them to achieve? Salespeople often fear setting goals too high; they may not attain them. They fear setting them too low because they may be fired. Who *owns* your goals?

A goal must be tied to a realistic vision. A goal without a vision is just a suggestion. I was setting goals without a vision and I was judging my success or failure by daily tasks. Then, it dawned on me. I was focusing on the task and not the vision! I needed to have the *why* clear to me. If you have a big enough *why*, you will always find the *how*. I decided to focus on the outcome, how I would feel and who I was capable of becoming. Did I want to become more spiritually in tune with my Maker? Who understands my potential better than He? Would spending daily time with the "Good Book" move me closer to being more closely aligned with God's purpose for me?

I remembered Coach Wooden's advice. Being a high achiever and a chronic "quick start," I failed to heed his priceless words of wisdom: "Focus on taking just a small step each day." I wanted to take gigantic steps, not baby steps. But if the existing conditions were not perfect, I would put off the gigantic step until I had more time or the conditions were just right. Like a bolt of lightning, it hit me. The key was to get into motion. A law of physics states that an object in motion tends to stay in motion. I decided to focus on getting into motion rather than on taking gigantic steps. Instead of reading a certain number of pages, I asked myself: *What step can I take this day that will move me closer to my vision?*

I committed to read one verse every day to move me toward my vision. I could easily take this step each day, and I would be reinforced by positive emotions resulting from my progress. How long does it take to read one verse of scripture? Half a minute? Bingo! Step attained and progress noted.

I discovered that once I was in motion, I often reached beyond the minimum set mark. The obstacle was not the number of pages; it was merely opening the book, and getting into motion! It truly was like Pringles potato chips. Who opens up a can of Pringles and eats only one potato chip? It's nearly impossible. When it comes to Pringles, most of us are over-achievers. The same is true when we have a clear vision, and we take baby steps towards that vision. It often turns out that we take more steps than intended. The difficult part is *getting into motion.*

For over ten years I have "pringled" the scriptures daily. My focus is on motion, and my steady achievements positively reinforce my vision. I have never read just one verse. Remember, once in motion you will tend to remain in motion. The purpose of a goal is not to serve as a target for some distant date; the most efficient use of a goal is simply to set you in motion. Find your Pringle that will get you into motion towards your desired intentions.

A few years ago, I read a great book entitled *Younger Next Year*, by Chris Crowley and Henry S. Lodge, M.D. This is a wonderful book—highly informative and motivational. They recommend that men over forty years old work out no less than forty-five minutes, six days a week for the rest of their lives. I was motivated! I wanted to get younger year after year, so I followed their advice: I woke up every morning and asked myself if I want to grow today, or do I want to decay today? I would say this question is highly motivational, wouldn't you?

Unconsciously, however, I ignored Coach Wooden's advice, and I set a "goal" to work out for at least forty-five minutes daily. You can probably guess the rest of the story. I missed a day; then, a couple of weeks later, I missed two days in a row. This cycle went on for a couple of months. Yes, I was feeling better, and I think I looked better, but I kept missing days and beating myself up for it every time. Finally, while traveling, I missed a whole week plus a few days. In retrospect, I guess I decided to start over at that point; I just didn't decide exactly *when* I would start over. In the meantime, I was losing my confidence.

Then, it dawned on me: I was blaming myself. I remembered what Deming said: "Ninety-four percent of all failure is a result of the system." I remembered Coach Wooden's advice about small steps and the Pringle

Theory. I needed to establish my vision, visit it frequently, and then just get myself into Pringle-like motion.

I envisioned myself physically fit, in the best shape of my life. I learned my lesson; Instead of committing to a goal of working out an hour a day, I first focused on the "why." I actually took time each day to visualize myself fit. I got in touch with how I would feel, how I would look and the things I would be able to do. To establish my vision, I literally get in touch with the sensation of confidence as I progress toward the vision.

What step can I take today to move me toward my vision? How about doing one pushup. One measly get-down-on-the-floor pushup. If I'm going to do that, I probably want to get into my workout clothes first. You don't see too many fitness experts advocating a pushup in street shoes. So, the small step that I can take today to move closer to my vision of being in great physical shape becomes: I declare that, just for today, I am going to put on my workout clothes and do one pushup.

Whether I am at home or on the road, that simple step has overcome virtually all of the obstacles I throw in the path of my personal progress. This has made a huge difference in my ability to sustain my ambitions. Rather than having a dialogue with myself about whether there is enough time to get a good workout (and usually concluding that if I skipped today, I could make up for it tomorrow), I simply put on my workout clothes and do the one pushup. But then I get "pringled." I might as well do a few more, and soon ten minutes have passed, and I generally reason that I could *probably* fit in another ten minutes, and before I know it, I have been working out for over thirty minutes, and often fit in much more!

I can assure you since I rethought my approach to goals I have never shown up at a gym dressed in my workout gear, done one pushup and hit the sauna. I hit the treadmill, the weights, whatever I felt like doing on that particular day. And what about those intermittent days when my workout only lasts a short time? I celebrate that I am in motion and moving toward my vision of being in great shape. I'm no longer setting myself up for failure by telling myself that if I don't work out for a full hour, I haven't reached my goal. Instead, I am using my vision, and then my progress—the step of "one pushup"—as a means of getting myself in motion.

Goals exist to get us in motion. They serve no other purpose. Along the way toward your vision, think of steps and milestones. A "step" is the minimum activity or task that you can do each day to get into motion. "Milestones" are those indicators or achievements that let you know you are making progress toward your vision. Milestones are not destinations. They are important measurable guidelines that you pass along the way to your vision by staying in motion. I truly was working out about forty-five minutes per day—days that I previously would have put off until the proverbial "tomorrow." I have learned that tomorrow means "not this day." I continue to pass milestones along the way: Most consecutive days of workouts (excluding Sundays) and my body fat and blood pressure dropped. But most importantly, I feel great! Visualize your milestones. You will be amazed at how fast you pass them along your journey.

Unlike a goal, your vision is never quite attainable. Your vision is actually a mental construct created by you to define what an achievement might look like. For example, my vision of "being in shape" has changed as I change. If I stay in motion, my confidence increases and my vision of what I can achieve increases. In spite of several knee surgeries, my new vision includes running a marathon—something that was definitely not part of my original vision. I was happy to run a mile. As you move towards that vision, however, the vision continues to move as well, and progressively gets further refined in your mind. Just like the horizon, it's always in view, but as you move toward it, it continues to reset itself. You can't sneak up on the horizon. You can't get up before daybreak and wait for it to appear beneath your feet. It, like your vision, is merely a mental construct.

An income goal is another mental construct. What happens when you reach an income goal? Have you heard yourself say, "You know, if I could just make $75,000 (or whatever), I would be happy. I don't need to make a lot of money. That would pay all my bills and leave me some extra." Did your ideas change when you reached that goal? What income do you envision now? Whatever it is, as you move toward it, your mind will force you to seek new horizons. This is an automatic function that we are all born with. As we move towards our targets, gaining confidence along the way, our internal "vision creator" continues to reset itself. If we are not in motion, our minds are incapable of providing us with realistic new horizons.

As our vision evolves, so do the steps we take each day and the milestones we pass along the way. By following the method I'm suggesting, you will fill your life with positive daily affirmations, and you will be amazed (and thrilled) by the incredible progress you achieve!

Another Analogy

You can also think about your vision in terms of a sailboat. You might have a destination in mind, but until you leave the port it makes little sense to trim the sails. The best step toward progress for a sailor would be to simply pull up the anchor. *There's always something holding us back, some dead weight keeping us from getting where we want to go and something anchoring us into a position of inertia.* Whether we're attempting to read scripture, work out or sail, the real purpose of a goal is to liberate the anchor. This will happen when your vision is clear, your milestones have been identified and you are taking your simple daily steps. When you've done that, anything is possible. Don't think that you have to lift the anchor into the boat to get into motion. Many times that will paralyze you and you will wait until you have the time and energy to lift that huge anchor all the way. Quadrant Motion Theory suggests that you only have to lift that anchor an inch—just enough to get into motion. Motion is the key! So determine for yourself what the *least* you can do today is ... now! This moment! What can you do to lift your anchor *just* enough to get you into motion?

An excellent example of reasonable goals that will put you in motion comes from the classic business book *In Search of Excellence: Lessons from America's Best-Run Companies,* by Thomas J. Peters and Robert H. Waterman. These authors studied the most successful businesses in America to find out the best practices they employed so that other businesses could use them to their benefit. When they studied the IBM sales force, they discovered, much to their surprise, that IBM had the lowest sales quotas in the computer industry. Despite this fact, IBM's sales force out-sold all the other sales forces of all the other computer companies, and Waterman and Peters wanted to know how and why.

Let's say that you are competing with IBM, and you own the XYZ Computer Company. You say to yourself, "IBM's sales force is expected to sell $200,000 worth of computer equipment *every day*. We'll set the bar higher, so that we can sell more. We'll demand that our sales team sell half a million dollars worth of computer equipment every day."

Sounds great. The first day, the IBM and XYZ salespeople head off to make their first sales calls. By late morning, they both emerge with sales for a $100,000 worth of equipment. The IBM salesperson says, "Look at me! It's only 10:00 a.m., and I'm halfway to my daily quota!"

The XYZ computer salesperson is looking at his watch. "Uh-oh," he is saying, with a knot forming in his stomach. "I better keep selling at this pace or I'll never make my quota."

By one o'clock, they've both sold another $100,000 worth of computer equipment. The IBM salesperson has reached his quota for the day, and feels like a million bucks. The XYZ salesperson, by contrast, swallows hard and thinks, "Nothing better go wrong the rest of the day or I'll never reach my goal."

Who's got the positive mindset? Who is thinking proactively? Who's striving and thriving? Conversely, who's playing not to lose?

The IBM salesperson now has choices. He can keep on selling in excess of the goal, and get himself one step closer to that trip to Hawaii (or whatever the prize on the sales board might be that month); or, he might take the afternoon off to play 18 holes. If you're in sales, however, when you're "feeling it" and you're "in the zone," the last thing you want to do is play golf. The IBM person may skip lunch because he wants to keep on selling. The XYZ salesperson may skip lunch, but it will be because his stomach is tied in knots due to anxiety. He's thinking, "I don't have a minute to lose." He is going to have a very tense afternoon, and when you're feeling tense, it's awfully tough to sell.

IBM's low quota actually propelled its salesperson beyond his or her own expectations of performance. Instead of high quotas or "goals," we want to have a clearly defined *vision*. A vision allows us to see ourselves benefitting from the goal; how we attain the goal is secondary. We want to focus on the feeling we know we will have when that vision becomes a reality. This is why we went through the Clarity Experience in Chapter 8 and you identified Four Keys, one from each region of the Brower Quadrant. When you are striving to attain a vision, it's a lot more exciting and energizing than when you are fearful that you may not reach a particular goal. It's all about knowing your vision.

The great motivator Earl Nightingale illustrated this with an example of a ship's captain. You could approach a ship's captain in any harbor and ask him how he was going to make it to his next port of call. He would tell you calmly and confidently that as long as he did the same simple things every day, he knew that he would reach his destination, even though he would not see land for ninety-nine percent of his journey.

When we have a vision, we grow confident because we know that as long as we keep taking the necessary actions, our vision *will* become a reality—even though there may be no direct evidence that the vision will come to fruition.

In his book *The Laws of Lifetime Growth: Always Make Your Future Bigger Than Your Past*, Dan Sullivan quotes Elizabeth Moss Kantor who says, "Everything looks like a failure halfway through." You may not *feel* like a great Bible scholar when you read just one line of scripture a day. You may not *feel* like a world-class athlete when you commit to just a single pushup. And you may not *feel* like a superior salesperson when you set low quotas for yourself. But when we set expectations for ourselves that are easily met, we find it equally easy to exceed those expectations. When we set the bar too high, we set ourselves up for frustration. Establish a high vision, visualize yourself there—actually having achieved it—and then ask yourself what small step can you take today. When you take that step, celebrate. When you exceed that step, really celebrate. Imagine how great you will feel as you stay in motion.

I find it fascinating that once we attain a goal or a desire, it isn't long before we take the accomplishment for granted, as if it had always been there or never really mattered to us. Noted American psychologist Abraham Maslow suggests that this is human nature: As we ascend each rung of the hierarchy of human needs, we take for granted the issues that the previous rung presented. Once we move past survival mode, we no longer even have thoughts of how to survive, even though just putting bread on the table might previously have consumed our every waking thought.

For this reason, we can expect to pass our milestones without too much fuss or fanfare. Statistical measures of success are not reasons to stop moving forward. The last thing we ever want to do is tell ourselves that we've "arrived"; we want to be continuously striving and thriving throughout our lives. We want to acknowledge the mile markers we pass. We might even get out of the car and take a picture of ourselves standing next to one, but we want to get back in our vehicle and continue along the Road of Predictable Results.

Daily Application of Vision and Steps

How many of you are to-do list makers? Do your co-workers or employees work from a to-do list? I had an assistant who would frequently write down at least one task that she had already done just so she could check it off! I occasionally make a to-do list, and it does feel good to check off the items. Experts say that you actually get a rush of endorphins merely by checking off one task on your to-do list.

I have also discovered, however, that in the quest for those endorphins, some of us attack the easiest tasks first, leaving the more important items for tomorrow. The easy tasks may be important, but perhaps not as essential as the ones we defer. It is not uncommon to get caught up doing *very important* things at the expense of the *essential*. (It's *essential* that we know the difference!) We may rationalize that tomorrow we can give the essential task the attention it needs and go home feeling great about all of the items we checked off our list today. Essential tasks are often put off beyond tomorrow and the "next" tomorrow, until they become a crisis. Then, finally, they get handled, but often in an environment of compromised confidence because we've been dragging our feet so long. Many times we end up asking ourselves why we didn't just do these tasks earlier and avoid all of the last-minute hassle. Be careful—here's an area where we can move ourselves from feeling guilty into a paralyzing sense of shame.

At Quadrant Living, LLC, we have implemented a practice to make sure we keep first things first. Each day, we each ask ourselves the following question: "If just for today I could accomplish only one thing, what would be the most meaningful task (step) I could complete that would move me (us) closer to my (our) vision?"

Once we have identified the one thing, we repeat the process until we pinpoint a total of *no more than the four most consequential steps for the day*; then, we immediately attack just those four steps before we even look at our to-do lists (if we have them). We have discovered that because we are in motion (even if it's just a Pringle), the essential things are getting done first, oftentimes before lunch, which is a huge advantage. Try it today:

Visualize your ideal result (your vision).

Now, ask yourself, "What one small thing can I do today that will move me toward my vision?"

Reading one verse of scripture may lead to reading pages; one pushup may lead to a forty-five minute workout; solving one problem of homework leads to completing an assignment; one phone call can lead to a series of actions. What is the one small thing you will do today that will move you toward your vision?

chapter 11

the empowered
quadrant bank

*The beauty of The
Empowered Quadrant Bank
is that it preserves a family's
sense of mutual obligation and
connection by maintaining a
feeling of interdependence.*

A few months after my "What's a guy like you worth?" experience mentioned in Chapter 1, I traveled to San Francisco for a meeting with a group of potential clients whom we'll call the Scarlatti family. The heads of the Scarlatti family, then in their forties and fifties, owned and operated one of the best known wineries in the Napa Valley, the lush wine region north of the Bay Area. They were one of those rare examples of a family whose business—and wealth—had survived the perilous passing to a third generation.

Their father, a member of the second generation of Scarlattis to live in America, had recently passed away and they were beginning to experience the effects of a family going from "we" to "me," from "What can we … (do, create, imagine together)" to "What's in it for me?"

There were four siblings, each with a different intention. The oldest daughter was the CEO and desired to keep the company and all of its holdings together. The oldest son, Eric, had a PhD in enology, the study of wine making. He was not really interested in running a business; he wanted to carve out the best vineyard for himself so he could continue to experiment with new wines. One of the other siblings wanted to liquidate his portion of the estate and make movies. The youngest was devoted to the arts and preserving the ecology of the planet. She also wanted to sell the business so that she could use the money to buy secluded mountain land and establish a retreat.

My task was to see if we could bring the family back to a "we" mindset by resolving their differences while allowing each member to thrive using his or her unique ability and passion.

We sat in a stunning boardroom overlooking rolling hills of beautiful vineyards. Early in the meeting, the siblings' mother shared the history of the family business. She told how their grandfather (her father-in-law), Angelo Scarlatti, had traveled from Italy to Northern California to make a better life for himself and his family. In Napa Valley, he found soil remarkably similar to the best vineyards in Southern Italy, from which his family hailed. So, Angelo did the only thing that made sense to him:

He bought a round-trip ticket to Italy so that he could bring back some grapevines and begin a new winery in California. After all, winemaking had been the Scarlatti family business for generations in Italy. It was what he knew best.

How Angelo managed to keep those grapevines in one piece as he made the trip back from Italy—across the Atlantic, through the newly opened Panama Canal, and up the west coast of the American continent—was anyone's guess; but somehow those vines survived the arduous journey, as did Angelo. The vines took root in the lush Napa soil, and an American family legacy was born.

"Wow, you mean Grandpa started all of this with vines that he brought from Italy in his pocket?" remarked the future filmmaker.

I was somewhat surprised that the fascinating history of the family vineyard was not well known by the younger members of the family. I posed a question. "When you think about all your family has acquired over the years—assets of many kinds—what do you consider to be your family's greatest asset?"

Eric Scarlatti, grandson of founder Angelo, thought for a moment. "The vines," he replied, sounding very confident as he gazed out the window at the vista of land, vines, machinery and workers. "After all, without the Scarlatti vines, there would be no Scarlatti wines."

"The vines are very important," I agreed. "But what about your Core Assets—you, your children and their children? Are the vines more important than the individual health, happiness and well-being of your family members?"

Eric admitted that he had not been thinking in those terms. "Certainly, the vines were not as valuable as the individual well-being of our family. You could always find a way to make a living, but not everybody finds a way to make a great life with his or her family members."

I addressed all of the Scarlatti grandchildren. "Okay, after the Core Assets of each family member, what do you believe is the next most important asset that your family possesses?"

The siblings looked at each other and scratched their heads. "It *has* to be the vines," Eric said, a little less confidently.

"The vines are very important, but what about the knowledge that Angelo brought with him and transmitted down through the generations—how to care for the vines once they were planted in the ground? What about the developed intuitive sense for harvesting the grapes? What about the network of relationships in the wine industry that Angelo and your father have cultivated as carefully as the vines themselves? What about the secret 'recipes' he concocted for creating such wonderful wines? What good are the vines if you don't know how to care for them once they are planted, or if you don't know how to make wine once the vineyards have been established? Or you've made the wine, but haven't established networks for marketing and distribution?"

The siblings acknowledged they had never thought of it that way. Certainly the vines were essential; but even more important were the Experience Assets—the knowledge and experience acquired and networks subsequently formed. These assets of wisdom and relationships might allow them to have used some other vines, and they might have developed an equally successful vineyard. "After your Core and Experience Assets, what's the next most valuable asset your family possesses?"

A longer pause ensued. None of the Scarlattis wanted to come up with the wrong answer. "The vines?" Eric timidly suggested.

"Okay, the vines. When we started this discussion, you may have thought that the vines your grandfather brought from Italy were the greatest treasure in your family. But what's truly unique about you as a family is what all of you have managed to do with what he brought back, while still maintaining great relationships for three generations. These are your most important assets."

"But after that it's the vines, right?" Eric teased.

"After all that, it's the vines," I agreed. We all shared a good laugh.

We then summarized that the Scarlattis have three types of assets: Core Assets, including the health, happiness and well-being of the family members; Experience Assets, including the knowledge of how to produce and market fine wines; and Financial Assets, including the vines and the winery. Additionally, over the years the Scarlattis have developed a rich tradition of giving. These Contribution Assets have become the glue that holds the family together, binding generations with a sense of purpose and accomplishment as they focus on improving their community. When families take the time to realize that perhaps their most valuable assets are those assets that are left after the money is gone, they are instilled with a new sense of purpose that drives them to discover ways to optimize all of their assets—not just their financial assets.

You are rich in so many ways. Have you done an inventory of all of your assets? Are you capturing your most valuable assets and systematically protecting them for future use? To do so requires a system that will bank all of your assets for future access for family members and others. Imagine having all of your family's true assets available to you—knowledge, wisdom, relationships, networks, methods, values, traditions, stories, encouragement and help. We would never have "to reinvent the wheel" again. Does such a system exist?

The Empowered Quadrant Bank

What do you think of when you hear the word "bank"? Most people think of it as a repository for the withdrawal and deposit of money. The Empowered Quadrant Bank (Q-Bank) is not only a repository for the deposit and withdrawal of Financial Assets, but of Core, Contribution and Experience Assets as well. The Q-Bank serves to formalize relationships in the family. In some families, because of the size and complexity of their financial holdings, the Q-Bank may have an innovative legal structure that supports and protects it. Let's face it. The erosion or loss of our Financial Assets can impact our Core, Experience and Contribution Assets. So, we desire a structure that offers the greatest protection from frivolous lawsuits, taxes and other unintended consequences. This might be in the form of a Limited Liability Company (LLC), a partnership, a trust or a corporation. In some cases, it might involve sophisticated offshore trusts for situational asset protection. The reasoning behind this is to create one or more legal entities capable of holding and protecting Financial Assets, sometimes in perpetuity. Just as a well-run corporation or bank outlives its founders, often by many generations, so a Q-Bank can be a vehicle for holding your family's most treasured assets—financial and otherwise—in trust for future generations. Even families that have not yet achieved a level of financial wealth sufficient to require the structuring of a legal entity like an LLC can create an Empowered Q-Bank in terms of concept and operation, without resorting to sophisticated structures. Be prepared, though. Families that start Empowered Quadrant Banks at any level and properly employ Q-Bank concepts are quite likely to end up wealthy enough to require the services of wealth-management professionals before too long!

The first question you want to ask when you create your Q-Bank is: *What does our family stand for?* What maxim best describes your family's ideology?

This is an exercise to determine and "capture" your values, an opportunity to capture in words the nature of your family's philosophy. This statement can represent either your historical approach to life or the approach that you and your family would like to adopt in the future. It can be fun to condense your philosophy into a slogan so that everyone in the family can easily remember and recite it.

In the Brower family, we asked each member to take a piece of paper and answer the question: What is a Brower? Answers ranged from four sentences to four pages. We then worked together to "drill down" the answers into one agreed-upon paragraph. We took it a step further, condensing the paragraph into one sentence and then down to one word. The word we selected was *powerful*! This was not accomplished in one evening. It took several attempts in which everyone rolled up their sleeves and ultimately agreed. We have since had great t-shirts made: "Brower Power," "Never Underestimate the Power of a Brower" and "Browers are Powerful." For us, "Powerful" is an acronym for: Prayerful, Obedient, Worthy, Eternal, Reverent, Forthright, Understanding and Loving. This is our guiding coat of arms—words and concepts that our family values the most. Over the years, we have added a few other acronyms that acknowledge our family philosophy as our family has grown and changed. What about your family? What does your family "stand for"?

The next step in creating your Q-Bank is to engage the entire family in the clarity exercise discussed earlier in Chapter 8. This is when you take stock of *all* of your family's assets and list them within the context of the Brower Quadrant. Each member of the family possesses assets in each of the four regions of the Brower Quadrant. This is a time to capture these assets *on paper*, so that you have a map of where the family is now. It's more than likely that you and your children—especially your children—will be pleasantly surprised by the variety, depth and strength of the assets they already possess in each of the quadrants.

In our society, we have a tendency to associate our worth as human beings with our financial net worth. The Q-Bank helps individuals and families recognize that they are worth far more than how much or little exists in their Financial Assets quadrant. The self-awareness and self-esteem generated by this process cannot be underestimated, especially for children. Our family meets at least once per year to evaluate the growth in each asset category. At this meeting, we answer these questions:

Have the assets in each quadrant increased or decreased since the last time we met?

What has changed?

What is our vision of where each of us will be the next time we meet?

This is where a family creates its vision for the future. Many times it is as simple as predicting our achievements in our various priorities of life. We return to the concept of the Four Keys, as presented in Chapter 8, Creating Clarity: What is the one area in which the family as a whole, and also each of us as individuals, would like to increase the asset value *in each of the four quadrants*? If the family were to meet one year from now, what would have happened in the meantime that would allow the family members to celebrate the increase in the combined family asset value? In this setting, I prefer to use a one-year time frame or shorter. This will vary with each family, but we want the time to be short enough so that we can almost *feel* it.

For example, perhaps the Core Asset key is health related, in which case the family might choose to increase its awareness of and commitment to healthy eating and exercise. In the Contribution quadrant, the family might commit to a new level of involvement with charitable, religious or similar entities. In the Experience quadrant, the family might decide to plan a trip to a distant part of the world to learn something new. Regarding the Financial quadrant, an adolescent may commit to earn enough money to buy a desired object, or perhaps the family as a whole could commit to saving money to buy something that would benefit everyone, such as a boat or a trailer. The number of choices is unlimited. Most families that utilize this system will align their one-year intentions with their larger view of who and what they are capable of becoming.

As we create our Empowered Quadrant Bank, we continue to utilize the concepts discussed throughout this book: moving from reactivity to proactivity, from management to leadership, and from negativity to a positive attitude. We are seizing the day and setting the course, instead of drifting aimlessly. It's amazing to hear an eight-year-old child at his second family meeting report about deposits he has made into their family Empowered Q-Bank because of his improved health habits. (It's practically a miracle to hear a teenager saying something equally positive about his or her contributions.) These are the wonders that await you when you create your own Empowered Q-Bank.

Q-Bank Asset Appreciation

The Empowered Quadrant Bank extends beyond legal documents or the yellow pad on which you have written your family's responses to the previous questions. The concept of increasing the value of all of your Q-Bank assets will impact future decisions. Because you have a new theory, you will ask different questions. Different questions will give you different answers, which lead to new and different results. You will begin to ask yourself, "How does this purchase, this vacation, this business or any other activity, opportunity or pursuit increase the true asset value of my (our) Q-Bank?" It's a medium for decision-making that has proved extremely effective in helping families decide how to optimize their time, efforts and the value of their True Wealth Assets.

When faced with the question of "What is the best choice for me (us) that is in alignment with my (our) vision or purpose?" consider the following questions:

What is the desired outcome?

Is this opportunity, activity or purchase in line with our values?

Will it make use of, or even improve, our unique abilities as individuals and as a family? Will it make us better?

How can the experience be *captured* as an asset, so that what we learn from it is even greater and longer lasting than the experience itself?

How will it benefit society?

Does it make sense financially?

An example of using these questions in decision-making comes from my own family's experience:

When our daughter, Kelsey, turned ten, we wanted her to experience more than the typical birthday—a party with several girls bearing gifts of lip gloss, fingernail decals and fragrant lotion. As we pondered for a philanthropic theme, an opportunity presented itself when two young college students were looking for donations through The Empowered Wealth Foundation to support their upcoming month-long mission working for an orphanage in Ghana, earning twenty-three college credit hours. A thought occurred that perhaps the young children in Ghana could use some supplies. A resounding "YES, please!" prompted our solution to Kelsey's party theme.

Invitations were sent out inviting the girls to Kelsey's roller skating party, complete with cake and ice cream (as well as presents from the family), but with a twist. We asked the parents to bring gifts for the orphans—unwrapped and appropriate for ages under five. Our dining room table soon brimmed with an abundance of soccer balls, stuffed animals, crayons, coloring books, etc. To take this a step further, Nick and Carly, an older brother and sister, donated their savings (matched dollar for dollar by my wife and me) to purchase ten backpacks and additional supplies so that each backpack contained a stuffed animal, ball, coloring books and crayons, writing tablets and basic reading books. Our three children personally delivered the backpacks to the two college students the day before they headed off to Ghana.

When the students returned, we hosted an open house at our office and invited all those who had helped raise money for the trip to Africa. The young women had prepared a beautiful slideshow of pictures and tearfully shared their moving experiences. During the slideshow, our children got to see pictures of the orphans wearing the backpacks, coloring in their new books and playing soccer. The impact of their generosity was immediate and profound. I don't remember my tenth birthday, but I don't think any of us will forget Kelsey's.

The decision to do this was in line with our family's values; it contributed to society and created a memory that lasts to this day. Now, it has also been shared with you— you might want to suggest a similar idea for your child or grandchild's next birthday. There are many ways you can put this type of tradition into effect, thereby creating a means of transferring not only your financial wealth, but also your values, to future generations. This is what the Brower Quadrant is all about.

Here's another way to put the Empowered Quadrant Bank to work: Let's say twenty-one-year-old Johnny is a newly minted college graduate. His college records indicate that he majored in economics, but anybody who knows Johnny understands that he majored in skateboarding. Johnny spent every waking moment at the skateboard park, perfecting moves, jamming on the half-pipe, doing ten-eighties for an appreciative audience, building and rebuilding skateboards, and otherwise living and breathing the skateboarding culture.

Johnny has an idea for a safety device that will take much of the risk out of some of the daredevil moves that have resulted in sprained and broken limbs. He has perfected this device, but doesn't want to sell it to a skateboarding company. Instead, he wants to start his own business, marketing skateboards with this new safety feature.

Johnny convenes a meeting of his family's Empowered Quadrant Bank. He explains that he wants to borrow $20,000 to get the business off the ground. The family applies the six questions above to Johnny's request. The desired outcome is that Johnny establishes himself as a business owner and creates self-sufficiency.

Is the opportunity in line with the family's values? It's certainly an act of service: If the company succeeds, Johnny will save countless young people trips to the emergency room.

Will it make use of the family's unique abilities? Yes, because one of Johnny's unique abilities is skateboarding; another is to identify a problem and a solution which others are willing to pay for.

How can the experience be captured as an asset? Johnny can document his experiences in starting and managing a business so that other family members can leverage off of his successes and failures. Johnny's entrepreneurial experience will keep other family members from having to reinvent the wheel should they decide to start their own business.

How will it benefit society? Fewer skateboarding injuries equals fewer dollars spent on medical care and a lot less pain. Additionally, Johnny has allocated a percentage of profits to promote workshops on skateboarding for underprivileged youth.

Does it make sense financially? If the business plan is complete and sound, and if the family can afford the investment, then the answer is yes—and a new business endeavor is launched.

If the business succeeds, Johnny will be able to repay his family's investment many times over. Even if it fails, the knowledge that Johnny—and his family—derives from the experience will be invaluable. Many business-owners fail with their first ventures but learn enough to make subsequent ventures succeed. In other words, Johnny and his family can't lose. This investment would be a sensible withdrawal from the family Empowered Q-Bank.

Assuming Johnny's parents are in their late forties or early fifties, they could have followed traditional estate-planning principles and kept that money locked up and out of sight until they pass away. By this time Johnny, statistically, would have been close to or even beyond traditional retirement age. The Empowered Quadrant Bank allows families to grow closer by making better use of their assets without waiting for death to trigger a distribution. With the skateboarding business launched, Johnny will be much more economically self-sufficient than if he had played the waiting game, "hanging out" in life until he received a bequest. It's easy to see the value of the Empowered Quadrant Bank under these circumstances.

Another example involving a real estate transaction follows. A daughter has married a young man who is just about to complete college. They qualify for a modest home loan. Shortly after buying a home, a friend suggests they purchase a parcel of real estate behind them and develop it. They like the idea, so they put some numbers together and present the plan to their parents.

The first question from the parents was: Has anyone in our family ever done this before, and if so, have they made a deposit into the Q-Bank of the knowledge they acquired in doing so? The answer was no. The couple was sent back to the drawing board.

Soon after, they were introduced to a friend of the family who was a real estate developer. He mentored this young couple and helped them refine their plan. The couple returned to the parents and explained that they had "borrowed the experience" they needed from their new friend and felt confident that they now had an experience-based plan that would create financial success. They could now answer one of the parents' questions: How will this improve the financial asset value of our family Q-Bank?

The parents, who had been very successful financially and were quite well known for their work, then asked the young couple how this experience would improve the Q-Bank's Core Asset value? After a few moments of thought, the daughter, wise beyond her years, replied that she had grown up in the shadow of her parents and completing this project would provide a huge boost of confidence and self-esteem.

Next, they were asked how this endeavor would increase the Experience Asset value of the family's Q-Bank. The couple replied that since no one had previously made a deposit of the intellectual Experience Asset for real estate development, they would make sure to deposit this acquired knowledge and make it available for other family members in the future.

Finally, they were asked how this would increase the Q-Bank's Contribution Asset value. The son-in-law responded that they would be paying taxes. This was not the proactive solution the parents were looking for, so the couple went back to the drawing board.

Shortly thereafter, they discovered a shelter for battered women located near the property they intended to develop. The shelter had a need for new beds and other equipment. The young couple took a tour of the facility and was excited to offer help. They would give a certain dollar amount from each lot they developed and sold to the shelter.

The parents looked at the proposed deal once again, and scored it, based upon the added True Wealth value. In its current form, the arrangement increased the value in all quadrants. Thus, they loaned the money to the couple at a very low interest rate plus an additional dollar amount for each lot sold. This would increase the financial asset of the bank for other family members who were not benefiting directly from this experience.

Approximately fourteen months later, at a family retreat, the young couple made a presentation to the family. As the daughter and son-in-law shared their experience, they noticed that Mom and Dad were taking notes. They were actually learning from their children's experience. What do you think that did for the couple's self-esteem and confidence?

The couple deposited a notebook and a CD, which outlined exactly how to develop a real estate project into the family Q-Bank. A younger sister and her husband later used that CD for their real estate projects and have added their deposits to the Empowered Quadrant Bank as well.

This young couple later presented to their family a letter from the shelter along with a newspaper article that featured their accomplishment. Their total gift was in excess of $14,000! The impact of their generosity widened as the shelter shared this experience with others, and successfully raised additional contributions to match the couple's contribution. Soon after came a check that paid off the loan to the Q-Bank; each asset category of the bank had increased in value.

This same concept worked, but for a completely different situation, when one of our children found herself in deep credit card debt. This was the first time she had lived away from home, and, by her own admission, she was not prepared for the onslaught of choices that were thrust upon her. We all have control over our choices when we reach adulthood; once we have made our choice, however, the consequences at times have control over us. She had come to the family Q-Bank for a loan. We did an assessment of how she was doing in each of the quadrants.

We first looked at her Core Assets: Did she have habits she needed to modify? Her Experience Assets: Did she lack experience in financial matters? Did she even know how to reconcile her checkbook? Her Contribution Assets: Was she participating in giving back? When she lived at home, she always contributed at least ten percent of her income to charitable causes. And, of course, when it came to her Financial Assets, she admitted that it was impossible for her to save if she was spending more than she earned!

We laid out a plan using the quadrants. She agreed to take the small steps necessary to create new habits that would improve her Core Assets. The bank arranged for a tutor to help her understand the nuances of reconciling a checkbook. She agreed to have an automatic withdrawal of ten percent of her salary go directly to a charity of her choice, as well as ten percent directly into savings. The Q-Bank then loaned her the money to consolidate her debts. And wisely, the Q-Bank also arranged to be paid through payroll deduction. What was the final score? A+ in each quadrant.

Many families have said that the Empowered Quadrant Bank is an excellent way to ensure that a family can transmit its values to its children, and therefore, to its grandchildren, and even great-grandchildren. If we do nothing to pass along our values, there is a significant chance that our values will never make it to the fourth generation. If you want to see your values reach the fourth generation, it's essential to create a system for passing along your values down through your future family. If you can see to it that your values and experiences will be transmitted four generations into the future, there is a very high likelihood that your values will continue to survive through the eighth generation and beyond. In fact, you can *bank* on it!

I was once told a story about a farmer whose tractor had fallen into a ditch. Spectators gathered as he hitched up an old blind mule to the tractor and then implored the mule to move forward in a most unusual way.

"Pull, Abigail! Pull, Jefferson! Pull, MacDonald! Pull, Warwick! Pull, Johnson!"

"What are you doing?" asked a puzzled onlooker. "There's only one mule there!"

The farmer nodded knowingly. "Warwick's blind," he whispered. "He doesn't know that there aren't any more mules around him. But he always pulls better if he thinks he's part of a team."

We are all a lot like Warwick. We all pull together when we feel that we're part of a team. As we will see in the following chapters, traditional estate planning tends to pull families apart, to turn them from "we" to "me." The beauty of the Empowered Quadrant Bank is that it preserves a family's sense of mutual obligation and connection by maintaining a sense of gratitude and interdependence. When a family pulls together, great things happen.

What does your family stand for?

What are the most important Core, Experience, Contribution and Financial Assets in your family's Empowered Quadrant Bank?

chapter 12

the five phases of wealth

"It has left me with nothing to hope for, with nothing definite to seek or strive for. Inherited wealth is a real handicap to happiness."

William K. "Billy" Vanderbilt

Arthur T. Vanderbilt II recounts his family history with great clarity in *Fortune's Children: The Fall of the House of Vanderbilt.*

As a teenager, Cornelius began the building of his empire with a small raft, charging fares for transporting goods and supplies, and eventually passengers, on the Hudson River. From this humble beginning, financed by a loan from his mother, he thrived. By the time of his death in 1877, the "Commodore," as he was then commonly known, was the wealthiest person in the world.

Within thirty years of the Commodore's death, no member of his family was among the richest people in the United States. Forty-eight years after his death, one of his direct descendants died penniless.

"This fabled golden era, this special world of luxury and privilege that the Vanderbilts created lasted but a brief moment," Vanderbilt II wrote. Over-indulgence, reckless spending, and poorly advised investments all contributed to the decline of the power and dominance of the Vanderbilt dominion. New titans with names that included Rockefeller, Carnegie, Frick and Ford replaced the Vanderbilts.

The Commodore's grandson, William K. "Billy" Vanderbilt, perhaps summed up the reactive attitude of the heirs best when he said: "It has left me with nothing to hope for, with nothing definite to seek or strive for. Inherited wealth is a real handicap to happiness."

The real tragedy is that not only had the family fortune been lost to (and by) the Vanderbilt heirs, but the lessons and knowledge that produced the wealth had been lost as well. Commodore Vanderbilt was a man who, through ingenuity and shrewd business acumen, built a veritable empire from the most meager of circumstances. Yet, all the experience, wisdom and knowledge he acquired were never transferred to future generations. The end result was a family unprepared for protecting and insuring the perpetuation of their grand fortune. When 120 of the Commodore's descendants gathered at Vanderbilt University in 1973 for the first family reunion, there was not a millionaire among them.

This is exactly what happens in the vast majority of families that create great wealth. By the end of the third generation, the wealth completely dissipates. It is so common that this cycle has turned into a proverb: "Shirt sleeves to shirt sleeves in three generations." This occurrence is a worldwide phenomenon; in China, the adage is: "Rice paddy to rice paddy in three generations." This brittle generation, the third, is statistically the final possessor of family wealth.

What causes this to happen?

George Land's book *Grow or Die* provides a theoretical answer. Land looks at all living things from a biological growth-directed perspective. Life grows and reproduces by the assimilation of materials taken from the environment and transforms into either constituents of the organism and its offspring, or the development of special products that aid growth. Land points out, "Growth cannot occur independently—it requires interaction and interrelation between the growing thing and its environment."

He identifies four distinct phases of life in all biological forms. The first phase is the incubation stage, which he calls the "accretive" stage. Here the life form is attempting to survive and grow strong.

"The early years of an infant's life are devoted almost exclusively to the process of self-discovery and self-seeking growth," he writes. Based upon his research, he correlates the biological phases of life with the growth and development of businesses.

Our research of family wealth has identified five phases of True Wealth growth or development. These phases include Striving, Driving, Thriving, Arriving, and Diving. Each phase has the potential for the development or stagnation and eventual loss of financial wealth, initiative and effort.

Phases of Wealth

If you've ever been to St. Louis, you've probably taken a trip to the top of the Gateway Arch, which commemorates the importance of the city in the settling of the American West. The Arch rises 630 feet above the Mississippi River and stands seventy-five feet taller than the Washington Monument. Visitors ascend to the top of the Arch by traveling on a custom-built tram that can carry forty people at a time. It takes four minutes to rise to the top of the Arch, but only three minutes to descend to ground level.

The Gateway Arch beautifully symbolizes a common occurrence: the creation and, all too often, rapid dissipation, of family wealth. The climb to the top is long and arduous, the view from the top is spectacular, and the drop-off or return to earth happens all too quickly.

We can think of the Arch as a visual representation of the phases of wealth; its curve rises out of the ground, peaking at some point, leveling out and then plunging back to earth.

Cruising

Before we look at the Five Phases of Wealth, we need to examine a non-wealth stage. I refer to it as Cruising. Did you ever cruise Main Street when you were in high school? On any given weekend night across America, one can find carloads of teenagers starting at one of end of Main, cruising to the other. Then what do they do? They turn around and do it again. These cruisers would go back and forth, looking for adventure. Most times it simply led to boredom and frustration, sometimes to occasional trouble. This scenario demonstrates a now somewhat common definition of insanity: doing the same thing over and over and expecting different results.

Some people spend their entire lives mimicking this same, monotonous boomerang effect. Rich or poor, these people have programmed themselves to be Cruisers. They live their life in reaction, avoiding growth at all costs, unwilling to risk going beyond the imaginary boundaries that someone or something else has created for them. Perhaps you know people that live their lives in this manner.

Most Cruisers believe they have many good reasons for not going beyond these limits. Sometimes it is due to the situation into which they were born—either too rich or too poor. Some blame the job they have, or that they didn't get a good education, or that health problems prohibit it; some say it's the government's fault. Whatever the reason, they live the life of a Cruiser. Most are either victims of the past, afraid to step foot into the present, or wishful thinkers awaiting their entitled good fortune to take them to their dreams. Many are cynics, constantly criticizing without offering up real solutions. Some just figure that if they cruise Main Street long enough, *something* good will eventually happen to them. The achievement of wealth cannot occur until you leave your comfort zone. It is time to go beyond that mythical line on Main Street.

Phase I: Striving

"Strivers" are willing to go beyond the city limits in search of their passion. They begin their ascension along this arch many times, attempting over again to find the perfect vehicle, continuing to look for something better, something magical, the perfect "ride" that will scale

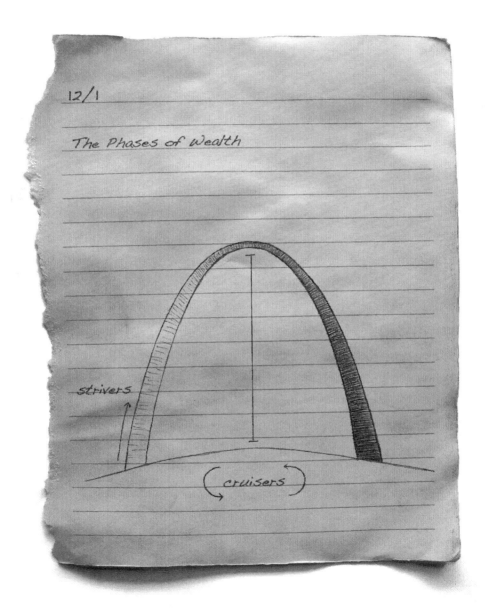

the arch of wealth. Occasionally, if not frequently, they proceed up the arch only to slide back down the left side and attempt to move up it once again. Some spend a lifetime striving to find the perfect vehicle. *Striving is a mandatory stage of growth.* How long we stay there is not mandated. It is up to you.

Unfortunately, there is a coterie of Strivers who are constantly searching—attempting but never sustaining, often jumping from one "get rich quick" opportunity to the next. The momentum of the chase increases with each revolution and results in a state of dizzy frustration like a dog that's been chasing its own tail.

Strivers, however, also desire more; they reach out beyond the boundaries of Main Street to discover a vehicle that will transport them to a life of greater meaning and reward. That vehicle may be a new job or career, education or an entrepreneurial opportunity. In this phase, creativity and hard work combine with the struggle of trial-and-error, resulting in a breakthrough, that some simply call "luck." Isn't luck where preparation meets opportunity? This can occur in a few years, or, in some cases, it can take generations.

If we are entrepreneurially minded, this is the phase in which our business begins. This phase is marked by numerous detours, false starts, twists and turns, moments of great excitement and moments of despair. If we are conscientious in this phase, our careers, businesses and families will succeed before long.

At the end of Phase I, people fully understand that wealth starts with finding their individual passion and developing their human (Core) and intellectual (Experience) capital. They have a broader personal and cultural perspective. Their human and intellectual capital is developed sufficiently to interact successfully with others. George Land theorized that the playful imagination of the child gives way to "realistic and mutual exchanges with others to create new ideas and information to increase his capabilities, not for himself alone, but for the group."

Wealth *transfer* has its own Phase I that is critical to wealth perpetuation. If the Striving phase is critical for the incubation of potential family wealth, it follows that the ingredients necessary to create the wealth in the first place are an integral component of how to perpetuate the wealth for future generations. *Ideally, it should be the intention of every first-generation wealth creator to honor and nourish that same opportunity of discovery, trial and error and development for every family member.* The objective is to discover and then nurture each child's unique gifts and abilities (their niche, so to speak), so that the child will not only survive, but also thrive.

In contrast to the Vanderbilts are the Rockefellers, who have been extraordinarily successful in certain aspects of perpetuating True Wealth. Since the founding of their fortune, the Rockefeller family successfully preserved its financial wealth. In the mid-nineteenth century, John David Rockefeller, Sr. created a fortune developing and using excellent business practices. He had the largest fortune in America at the time of his death. Unlike the Commodore, however, Rockefeller, Sr. recognized that his one son had no interest in business. Instead of forcing his son to enter the family business, he allowed his name-sake to find his own niche. This was an extraordinary act. He allowed John, Jr. to find his own passion and explore his own dreams. He allowed his only son to go through the process of self-discovery and self-seeking growth (the Striving phase). He supported his son in finding his own happiness. As James E. Hughes writes in *Family Wealth*, "this decision on the part of John Davison Rockefeller, Sr. to free his son to follow his individual pursuit of happiness is one of the most long-term wealth-preserving decisions in history."

When financial wealth is present, there is tremendous pressure to have the children follow in the footsteps of the family enterprise builders. If the "family business" has transitioned to a "business family," certain professions are encouraged by tradition. If True Wealth is to persist, however, the child's interests and strengths must be assessed, identified and encouraged. Ideally, this can be followed up with targeted education and mentoring.

To have the highest probability of successful wealth transfer, parents need to support the Striving process in their offspring. Ideally, this happens when the children are still living at home, but is successful with offspring that are much older. Age is not the primary success factor. What *is* primary is the willingness of both parents and children to acknowledge the need to experience the Striving process. Discovering each child's unique abilities and desires provides the deepest "gas tank" for the child. With plenty of fuel, children have the most energy to pursue their dreams. When they're not working within their unique ability, passion and interests, their gas tank is small, and even if they desire to please the family, eventually they will run out of gas and perform poorly. One of the greatest gifts that parents can give their children is to discover the child's passion and unique ability.

Phase II: Driving

It is at this point that the individual can move up the left-hand side of the Arch to Phase II—Driving. As individuals and families begin building their wealth, either through contracts or businesses, they reach a stage where they begin to feel like they have made it. This interim phase is accompanied by the beginnings of surplus. They can pay their bills, travel in style and move to a better neighborhood. They begin to enjoy a sense of financial stability that might have eluded them during the Striving phase. They may not be satisfied, but they no longer have the same financial pressures they once endured.

This is a growth stage. The wealth continues to grow. Originators get better at what they do, and are consequently rewarded for creating value. We are now *driving* the vehicle that we believe will take us up the Arch, the perfect career or business opportunity. Once we find that vehicle and we stick with it, improving it along the way, onward and upward we drive. Discovery in today's fast changing world is more about identifying your unique ability and then being able to apply it through various opportunities. It is not uncommon for someone who understands and has confidence in their unique ability to apply it with different companies and opportunities. Think of an athlete with unique skills. It is not uncommon for them to leave

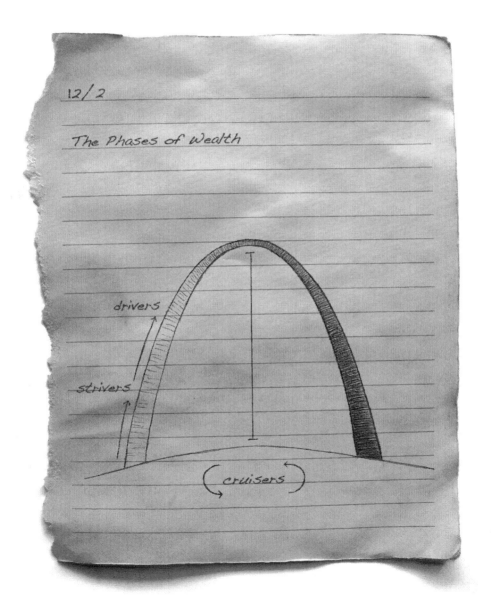

one opportunity for an even greater opportunity. Find your niche and then continue to improve the vehicle.

We are halfway up the Arch, and we have a sense for the first time that the top is within reach. What the "top" of the Arch is for one person might be different for another, but the feeling is the same: our vision is reachable. It's an exciting time to be alive.

Phase III: Thriving

To continue further up the Arch, we must enter the third phase—Thriving. Land calls this the "explicative" stage. In it, the "individual matures, mutualizes with, and contributes to the growth of a larger social organism." In this situation a person develops in a community of humans "in exactly the same way a cell community grows, and, if we look closely, evolves exactly the same functions: manufacturing, circulation, communication, protection, control and so forth."

The younger Rockefeller, in his Thriving phase, was just as productive in creating systems of family governance and philanthropy as his father was in business. John, Jr. set up a family office to manage the needs of his six children—one daughter and five sons. The system of family governance that he established continues today. It is this

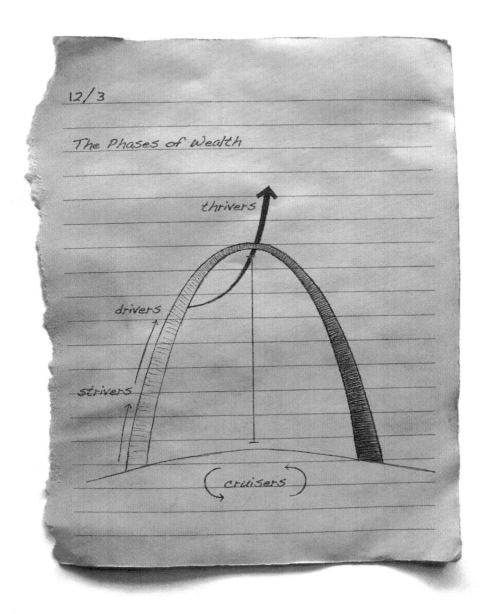

system that is credited with the long-term wealth of the Rockefeller's fourth, fifth and sixth generations. While its investment performance has been excellent generation after generation, its greatest value to the family is derived from its wealth of educational services. The Rockefeller's family mission is "to grow the human and intellectual capital of the family."

Like his father before him, John D. Rockefeller, Jr. encouraged each of his children to find their niche (Striving phase). He knew that supporting them in pursuing their individual happiness would lead them to productive, wealth-preserving lives. In his book, *Family Wealth,* James E. Hughes discusses the Rockefeller's success: "The resulting contributions of the third-generation Rockefellers to philanthropy, to government, to international banking, and to the birth of new industries through highly venturous investments are remarkable."

Thrivers have learned a very important key: They know how to replicate their success and transfer that wisdom to others, so that the business and lessons learned from their experiences achieve a life of their own and will actually outlive them! If you don't know how to replicate or capitalize your successes and haven't developed systems so that the knowledge and experience of the journey can out-live you, you simply remain in the Driving phase.

Perhaps you have a vehicle you can transfer to your heirs, but if you haven't taught them the secrets of successful driving, they will eventually wreck and possibly destroy the vehicle you worked so hard to find, build and drive. If you or your successors can't replicate the path that led to success, when your "vehicle" runs out of gas or needs repairs, you, too, begin that downward slide.

Thrivers see the top of the Arch and ignore the possible downward direction that path will take them. Rather, they continue building and contributing so that they remain on a skyward-bound path that continues for generations. Ideally, they exist as Thrivers forever, and never experience the other phases of wealth. They have developed systems that allow them to bypass the plateau and continue the climb. Instead of a bell curve, some Thrivers create their own Quadrant Living Power Curve. Fortunately some families have successfully maneuvered around the obstacles. In every community there are those few family enterprises that continue to thrive generation after generation. Unfortunately, this is often the exception. We read more about family enterprises that end in complete disarray, squabbling over and squandering unearned fortunes.

For most families, this phase of wealth has differing periods of sustainability. Typically, as one generation passes on, the succeeding generations are less equipped to handle the wealth. Once Thriving wanes—or even ceases—they are obliged to reside in the phase that has a slippery slope down the other side of the Arch. The Brower Quadrant systems are designed to assist you in maintaining a state of perpetual Thriving!

Phase IV: Arriving

Arriving is dangerous! An Arriving mentality can occur at any time. It doesn't necessarily follow Thriving. Some Drivers bypass the thriving phase altogether. If the fourth phase, Arriving, is reached, the individuals actually believe they have "arrived." In *Grow or Die,* Land explains that the individual frequently attempts to recreate "his own pattern to make the other person (his offspring) more like himself, not by direct control but in thought, deed, dress and so forth." The result is little or no growth. The relationship becomes "one of conformities in conflict." Both the wealth-creator and offspring attempt to change the other into their own pattern.

This is where growing stops and dying begins. Without the robust energy created by finding one's unique gifts and capabilities, the offspring are severely handicapped. This is where False Wealth hangs out. Many residents of the "Arriving" phase base their success upon a financial

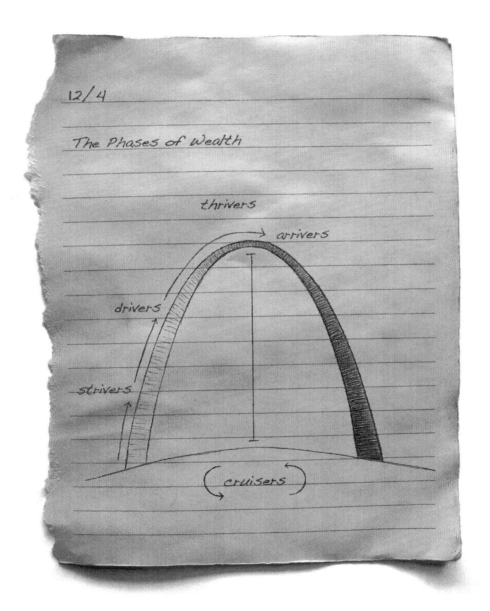

scorecard only. Lottery winners or football players who sign their first contracts with the NFL sometimes believe they have arrived. They are convinced that this sudden onslaught of financial wealth is the cure all and end all. But are they able to actually replicate this success or fortune? These individuals go from a state of financial struggle to multimillionaire status literally overnight. Are they Arrivers or Thrivers? They become Thrivers if they can actually replicate the wisdom of the experience that brought them their so-called success and transfer that wisdom to others-their heirs and successors. Otherwise, they detour without having reached the Thriving phase and leap into the Arriving phase.

People who "arrive" in a hurry seldom benefit from the Striving, Driving and even sometimes the Thriving phases. Do you have to be financially rich to enter the Arriving phase? By definition, you only have to stop creating. We now have third, fourth, fifth and sixth generation heirs of affluence who believe they are entitled simply because they had a Driving/Thriving ancestor. There are also multiple generations of the so-called "deprived" who also have a sense of entitlement simply because they have a rich uncle, Uncle Sam!

The Arrivers have entered into survival mode. Instead of being in a state of abundance, they operate from an assumption of scarcity. They are not contributors, but possessors and takers. They do not have open arms, but rather attempt to wrap their arms around all of their possessions, like a starving, insecure hermit sitting at a table, protecting his meal. Individuals in the Arriving (or "Surviving") phase are not playing to win, as are those who are Striving, Driving and Thriving.

People who receive a sudden influx of wealth without the knowledge of how to care for that wealth often find themselves in this survival category, lacking the confidence to replicate the success and abundance that was suddenly thrust upon them. By "playing not-to-lose," they are headed on a steep descent. They often don't know how to contribute to society and are afraid to part with their wealth because they don't know how to make it back. They follow rather than lead, copy rather than create. They usually do not experience the joy that comes from actualizing their own dreams and instead become frustrated and unhappy despite the vast financial wealth they possess. Those who tend to view themselves as having "arrived" at the top of their Arch, whether they've earned it through hard work or simply inherited it, slowly, subtly, and subconsciously begin the slippery slide down the other side of the Arch.

On the real Gateway Arch, it takes less time to reach the bottom than it did to reach the top. And so it is on our metaphorical wealth arch, as the plunge through the Arriving phase takes us down slope of the arch to the fifth phase, Diving.

Phase V: Diving

Without intervention in Phase IV, the family or the individual transitions into the next potential phase—Diving. Absent a system to educate, train, involve and assist family members, to actually think and act like first generation wealth builders, future generations are left to their own devises. They must recreate from scratch their own success context. Many individuals don't succeed on their own, without the tools, motivation and foundation. This is a pattern that repeats itself over and over again throughout the world.

In terms of family wealth, the creators of wealth are the Drivers and Thrivers, and their offspring or future generations, all too often, are Arrivers—individuals who were born on third base and actually believe they hit a triple. This attitude of entitlement cannot co-exist with an attitude of gratitude. Those living with ingratitude believe that they have not received everything to which they feel entitled. These individuals coast downward, giving truth

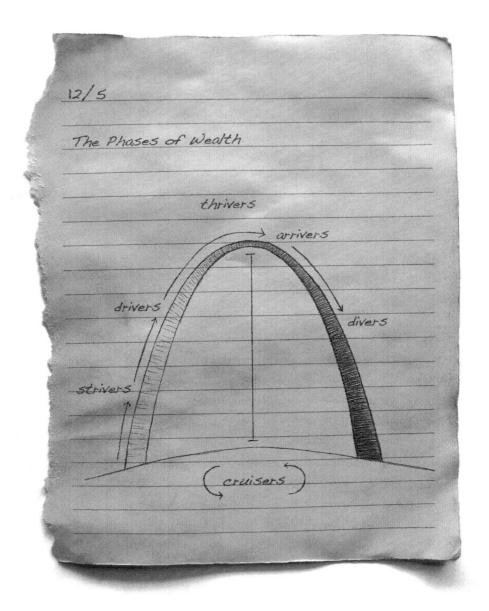

to the expression, "Shirtsleeves to shirtsleeves in three generations." Without the wisdom and experience gained in the Striving, Driving and Thriving phases, we all can be headed for a serious fall.

We certainly see this with NFL players and lottery winners—clear examples of people who have "arrived." We see the young men triumphant on the day they sign with their clubs. Suddenly, individuals who may never have had any Financial Assets are worth millions of dollars. Then, within three years of retirement, almost four out of five NFL players are either broke or divorced or both. Just because they *arrived* at a significant sum of money did not give them the ability to hold onto their wealth or grow it. The plunge from the top is swift and often played out in the media.

There have been surveys of lottery winners that show that wealth not only failed to improve their lives, but also actually destroyed their lives. The winners found themselves at odds with family members (many of whom they may have never met) who made demands to share in their newfound wealth. Communities treat them differently. Storeowners and service people may treat them differently, expecting more money simply because they have larger checking accounts. Friends fade away, fearing that they can't "keep up" with their newly affluent associates.

Many lottery winners, in fact, have had to leave their hometowns and start over in places where they—and their newfound wealth—were unknown.

Clearly, when it comes to the Gateway Arch, the best place to be is on the left side of the curve with the Drivers and Thrivers, instead of taking chances with the Arrivers and Divers. One group is playing to win and the other group, playing not-to-lose, has a doubtful shot of winning. Those on the ascending side take a proactive stance toward life; they are building, growing, doing, creating, and taking responsibility for their actions. Theirs is an attitude of *empowerment*. They are contributors. Those who see themselves at the top, and those who are careening down the right side of the Arch, are living in reaction and passivity. They do not *make* events happen, but are instead controlled by events. They seem to have an attitude of *entitlement*. They are the takers. They often lack the courage to shift back to the proactive side of the Arch. They are on the failing side of the metaphorical arch and they don't know what to do about it.

Which side of this power curve do you want to live on, the proactive or the reactive side?

Thanks to the wisdom and experience of clients and colleagues, and thirty years of ongoing research studying

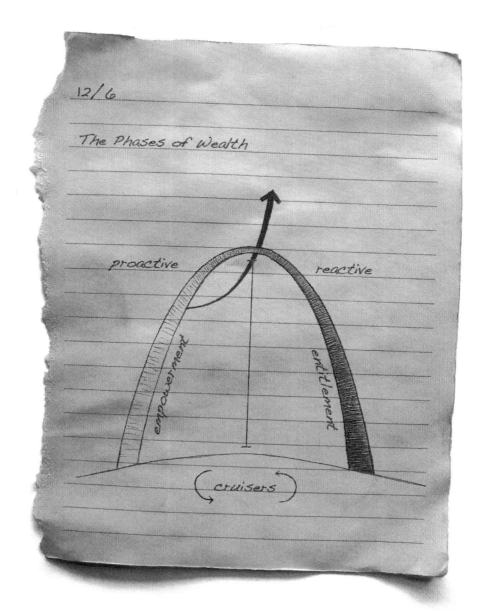

families from all economic stations in life, successful systems have been developed for discovering values, achieving clarity, balance, focus and confidence. In addition, methods of sharing these concepts with everyone in your zone of influence have emerged.

You are at the center. As your life is transformed by coming to understand the phases of True Wealth, you will be able to radiate your values outward toward your children, community and workplace, as well as toward future generations. It all begins with *you*.

What phase of wealth are you in?

What phase of wealth would you like to be in, and what steps can you take to move you toward that phase?

What are the unique interests of each of your children?

How might you help them achieve success in their fields of interest?

chapter 13

estate planning vs. family leadership

"If your actions inspire others to dream more, learn more, do more and become more, you are a leader."
John Quincy Adams

"Hey, Dad, can I have $10,000?" Dad looks up from his newspaper.

"What for, son?"

"What's the difference, Dad? You're rich! You can afford it!"

"What will you do to earn the money?"

"Nothing. I was hoping you'd just hand it over."

"What are you going to do with it when you get it?"

"I don't know. I guess whatever I want."

What are the chances that Dad's going to hand over the ten grand? It's highly unlikely. Would you hand over a large sum of money to your son or daughter without a plan that you believed in? Our level of confidence suffers without a plan. Like handing your car keys over to an aspiring Indy driver with no training, most would consider this gratuitous exchange to be pure folly. Perhaps the young man need only be patient because when his father dies, he'll get millions—possibly without even having lifted a finger.

Make sense? Let me pose a question. Which would you rather have—Tiger Woods' clubs and trophies, or Tiger Woods' course knowledge and swing?

Most people would choose the swing and course knowledge. After all, with the wisdom and experience, you can replicate all of the trophies and other "things." Yet, how many times do we see the heirs fighting over the metaphorical nine-iron or quibbling over who gets which trophy, etc. The cottage industry of estate planning has become very adept at efficiently (economically) dividing up the clubs and trophies amongst the heirs with very little regard to transferring the "swing"—which is to say, the intangible wisdom, values and relationship assets, to future generations. It may sound as if I'm criticizing the entire estate planning industry. It is not my intention to lay blame, but rather to point out the challenges that accompany the traditional path often chosen by family leaders to move their assets through the generations. This is a *systemic* issue. Heretofore, there have been no clearly defined systems that integrated and optimized the dynamic nature of *all* of the family assets—not just the financial. What is the philosophy underlying traditional estate planning? Beat the taxman, and, ultimately, dump all you can on your heirs, regardless of their ability to handle sudden wealth.

In a recent congressional debate over the need for estate and inheritance taxes, it was recorded that the estate planning industry has done more to destroy the American family than taxes ever will. How does this happen? It is not uncommon for estate planners to focus on wealth transfer without wealth responsibility. An heir to an estate can wipe out in a few years what took a lifetime to create. Dividing the money all too often ends up dividing the family. I once had the privilege of asking General Alexander Haig what he considered the first rule of war.

"Divide and conquer," he replied instantly.

Our research shows that traditional estate planning often intentionally divides (the wealth), which unintentionally destroys (the family). The transfer of wealth without responsibility is a recipe for destroying wealth—and, all too often, tearing a family apart. I call this phenomenon "disinterdigitization."

Think of your hands clasped firmly together with your fingers interlocked or "interdigitized." This is symbolic of the way a family should exist. Each finger is able to move independently of the other, but there is no question that together they are more solid, better protected and stronger. "Disinterdigitization" takes the family and their assets and pulls them apart, transforming the family from "we" to "me."

Passing along wealth without passing along the values and the wisdom is like giving your child the most phenomenal super computer in the world, minus a monitor. The computer has the power to solve any problem, but it's impossible to see what's going on as it does so, or to understand its motivation. That's an apt simile for passing along money without requiring accountability.

A few years ago, I flew to California for the funeral of my grandmother, a wonderful, loving woman. I loved our Sunday visits to her home when I was young, and can still recall the taste of the fried chicken she made—the best I ever ate. As an adult, I had not seen her nearly as often. At the funeral, I realized just how little I knew of her life. I learned there that during WWII, her husband (my grandfather) was quite ill, and it fell upon my grandmother to support the family while her sons served their country. Among other accomplishments, she was one of the first female postmasters in the nation. Her father had been appointed sheriff in a Texas town at age nineteen, the youngest sheriff in the history of Texas; apparently, he had to flee to California after a run-in with a criminal gang.

I didn't know any of these things before the funeral, and as I flew home, the fact gnawed at me: I had never taken the time to learn the lessons of my grandmother's life, how she coped with adversity, how she made her way and built a life for herself in tough times.

While I was thinking about these things on the flight back, the man sitting next to me, a jovial, older fellow interrupted my reverie. "What do you do?" he asked, in the bluff, hearty manner of the successful salesman.

Normally, I love to speak with people, learn about their lives and discover our commonalities and differences. But right then, I was still mourning not just the loss of my grandmother, but also the loss of the knowledge that she could have shared with me and the rest of her family, had we only thought to ask her about her life and capture her experiences.

My seatmate waited patiently for a response. I explained that I consulted with affluent families about how to transfer their most important assets to future generations. I tried to keep the conversation short.

"Oh, you mean estate planning!" he exclaimed happily. "I've done mine already!"

At that time, whenever anyone told me that they had "done" their estate planning, I used it as an opportunity to remind them that estate planning was a process, not an event. It is only done if you die the instant you put your pen to the paper. Changes in families, tax laws, circumstances, fortunes and misfortunes all demand that the planning and preparation continue. Estate planning without an ongoing system of adjustments and family preparation is like a ship's crew that declares their voyage a success simply by leaving the port. There is no such thing as "having it done"—another reason I feel it should be called "estate leadership." I didn't have the heart for such a discussion at that moment.

My companion told me how happy he was that he and his team of advisors had crafted a plan that provided for great financial wealth to be passed on to his children during and after his lifetime, so that they would enjoy it now without waiting for him to expire. As for his grandchildren, they truly were set for life. Their educations were paid for, money was set aside so that each would have a house shortly after graduating from college, and a considerable amount of money would be provided with which to start their adult lives.

I commended him both for his thoughtful planning and for his generous nature. As our conversation continued, however, something became clear to him: He may have been able to set his grandchildren up financially and remove all money worries from their lives; but, he realized, he wasn't set up to pass on to his grandchildren some of the most valuable experiences in his own life.

Neither his children nor his grandchildren would ever know what it was like to build a fortune from scratch, as he had. His grandchildren would never experience the hunger and drive to build and create as he had, which was a result of *not* having had all of his needs met early on. They would never have the intense satisfaction of taking financial responsibility for their own educations, for putting together the down payment on their homes, or for developing the discipline of learning to save and invest. They would never experience the self-respect that comes from making it on one's own. They would never have the opportunity to assist their own children with getting a college education because Grandpa had already done it for them

The jovial smile disappeared from my new friend's lips. "I've stolen from them," he said. "I'm a thief! In giving them everything, I've stolen from them what's most important." His confession caught me off guard. I had never thought of it in those terms. Perhaps he was right.

He assured me that as soon as the flight landed, he would get in touch with his financial advisors and together they would create a plan that gave his children a safety net, but not the entire amount that he'd previously laid out for them. My seatmate spent the rest of the flight formulating a plan that would not impede his children's growth into adulthood. When we parted, his words: "I've stolen from them!" were lodged in my brain. Do we get so caught up in efficiently avoiding the taxman and dividing up our estate that we deprive our children and grandchildren from experiencing some of the greatest joys of pride, self-esteem and accomplishment? There is a better way, but first we must step out of the proverbial box.

In Chapter 2, we noted the three greatest fears of today's wealth builders: loss of choice and control, fear that financial wealth might create negative outcomes for heirs, and the fear of leaving no lasting or empowering legacy.

Loss of Choice and Control

Imagine the effect when we withhold opportunities that would enable our children to experience the challenges and blessings from making their own choices. When we set up systems that allow our children and grandchildren to take ownership for their potential outcomes, we are preparing a generation of leaders. I have seen parents and grandparents who are truly preparing their children— giving them a sense of ownership rather than a stifling attitude of entitlement.

Imagine grandparents who establish systems that encourage education. For example, they may agree to match an educational savings account at the child and grandchild level. This allows everyone to participate together. Systems are created that encourage planning, self-discipline, thrift and savings at an early age. They take the little ones on field trips to universities and colleges to get them excited and view what college is like. Believe it or not, experiences like these create the context that make goals a true vision. A goal without a vision is just a suggestion or a recommendation. Vision creates ownership. They are proactively encouraging and preparing their heirs for the incredible value of an education. The children develop a sense of empowerment rather than entitlement. They make choices on how to prepare for education, where to go and what to study.

Contrast that with just giving them the money for education. An "Quadrant Living" family can accomplish so much more with a system that prepares, not just protects!

Creating Negative Outcomes

The second greatest fear of the affluent was creating negative outcomes for their heirs through inheritance. Here's a scenario that illustrates this point:

"Hey, Dad," says seventeen-year-old Junior. "I've got an idea. Why don't we go look at the new Porsches this afternoon?"

Dad, a self-made millionaire to whom all the clichés apply—looks up from reading the sports page. "Why do you suggest that, son?"

Junior shakes his head. "Dad, they're so *awesome,* and nobody at school has one. I've been driving that little BMW for over a year and everyone says that only preppies drive BMWs."

Junior's words sink in. They trigger a host of "When I was your age ..." lectures, none of which Dad chooses to deliver just now. "If you think for one second," Dad sputters, trying to keep a grip on his temper, "that your mom and I are going to buy you a new Porsche, you're out of your mind!"

"So, that's the way it works," Junior says. "You don't have enough money to make sure your son looks his best at school, but you've certainly got enough to make sure that you and Mom each drive the latest and most expensive Mercedes."

By now, Dad is fuming. "All you think about is yourself! If you want a Porsche so bad, why don't you get a job and buy one?"

"Let's see ... eight dollars an hour times ten thousand hours ... hey, I can buy a Porsche for myself in just five years—*if I quit school!*"

"When I was your age—"

"Spare me," Junior snarls. "You scrimped and saved to buy a '55 Chevy for twelve hundred dollars. Somehow you pulled the money together. I'm tired of that story. That was okay for you, Dad, but *your parents* weren't putting pressure on you to make good grades so you could go to Harvard and make something of yourself! Your parents probably didn't even care *if* you went to college, just as long as you could get a job somewhere. Times are different now, in case you haven't noticed!"

Dad is speechless. Junior turns on his heels and walks away. Father and son are equally angry.

A few weeks later, Mom and Dad discuss what to buy Junior for his birthday. Dad sheepishly suggests a new Porsche. In a feeble attempt to rationalize, he stated it will be good for his self-image, which will probably help him study harder so he can get into Harvard.

Mom is surprised at Dad's suggestion. Dad has always been preaching the virtues of earning what you get. Prying enough cash from his wallet to buy their son's BMW the previous year was an exercise in frustration that she never wanted to repeat. But if Dad is up for it, a Porsche it will be.

After the birthday party, Dad pulls Junior aside and reminds him that if he doesn't get good grades he'll lose the car. The only reason they're giving him the Porsche is because they wanted him to have a better self-image.

"This wasn't easy for us, son. Your mom and I had to sacrifice to buy this car for you."

The words ring hollow for Junior. The family lives in an 8,000-square-foot house and Mom and Dad drive the best and newest his-and-hers Mercedes. But Junior knows better than to bring up the obvious.

"You better get good grades and stay out of trouble. We expect you to get those grades and get into Harvard. You've got no excuses now."

"Thanks Dad. Thanks Mom. You guys are the greatest parents in the world!"

Now, here's my question for the reader: If you were a seventeen-year-old high school senior with keys to a Porsche jangling in your pocket, exactly how much studying would *you* get done?

You might be thinking that your family isn't like the Rockefellers or the Vanderbilts. Your family doesn't have that kind of money, so you shouldn't have those kinds of problems.

I beg to differ. This same issue—*the transfer of financial wealth without an accompanying transfer of values*—affects all of us.

Let's listen in on another family feud, one that takes place, with slight variations, in homes across the country, at every socioeconomic level, every day of the year.

"Mom! Dad!" the fifteen-year-old boy exclaims as he rushes into the house as dinner is served. "I've got great news! I made the varsity basketball team!"

"That's great, son!"

"There's only one problem: I need a new pair of basketball shoes."

"But we just bought you a pair a couple of months ago," Mom says.

"Yeah, and they cost eighty-five dollars," Dad says. "I never paid that much for a pair of shoes throughout my whole childhood, even with adjustment for inflation."

"You don't understand! Everybody else on the team has these cool new basketball shoes! They're called Air Stylus, and they're awesome! You guys were urging me to go out for the team, and I made it! Now you're not even going to support me?"

Mom and Dad exchange glances. A peaceful dinner is on the verge of turning into a battle. Dad swallows hard. "What's wrong with the basketball shoes we just bought you?" he asks.

Junior rolls his eyes. "*Daaaaaad*, nobody else is wearing those old things. Everyone's wearing Air Stylus. Even the coach. I wouldn't be part of the team."

"How much is this gesture of 'support' going to set us back?" Mom asks gingerly.

"Only a hundred and twenty dollars" the son says, eyes downcast.

"One hundred and twenty bucks?! Do you know how much it costs just to keep this family fed and taken care of? Why, your mother—"

"I know all about my mother. You told me to go out for the basketball team, and I made the basketball team. And everybody wears Air Stylus on the basketball team ... except me."

"Well, it is kind of tough for a boy not to fit in at his age," Mom says.

One look around the table indicates Dad's licked. "I guess we can do it," Dad says, but he still feels the need to instill a little guilt. "But I want you to know it means we're going to have to be late with the rent check this month."

A late rent check is of no concern to the boy. It means nothing to him. All that matters is that he is getting his one hundred and twenty dollar basketball shoes.

"Thanks, Dad! Thanks, Mom! You guys are the greatest parents in the world!"

Now let's look at the same scenario involving a Quadrant Living approach: Junior bursts into the dining room shouting, "Mom! Dad! I just made my high school basketball team!"

"That's great, son! We are so excited for you!"

"Yeah, but there's a problem. All the other kids wear these one hundred and twenty dollar basketball shoes. I feel kind of left out, if you know what I mean."

Dad nods. "I do know what you mean, son. How can we help?"

"You could buy me the same shoes all the other kids have—like I said, they're only one hundred and twenty bucks."

"We'll be happy to lend you the money, son," Dad says.

"*Lend?*" the boy says doubtfully. "Don't you mean *give?*"

"It works like this," Mom says. "If we just handed the money over to you, you'd get the basketball shoes, but you wouldn't really learn anything other than you can get something for nothing in life, and that's not a lesson your father and I want to teach you."

"That's right," Dad says. "So what we'd like you to do is tell us what you want to give us for collateral, some item of value that we'll hold until you pay back the hundred and twenty dollar loan."

"You mean you're not going to give me the money for the shoes unless I give you something of equal value?"

Mom and Dad nod.

"Like what?" the boy asks, "What do I have that has … value?"

Dad ponders the question for a moment. "How about your Nintendo®?"

Junior responds as if they've asked for a kidney. "You want my *Nintendo?*"

"We don't want it forever," Dad says. "We just want it until you pay back the money for the loan."

"I give you my Nintendo until I pay you back the money? Forget it. I won't do it."

"That's fine with us," Mom says. "In that case, you keep your Nintendo, and we'll keep our one hundred and twenty dollars. Pass the asparagus, please."

The boy sees his new Air Stylus basketball shoes slipping away. "Tell me again how this works," the boy says.

"It's like this," Dad begins. "You box up your Nintendo and give it to us. We'll give you one hundred and twenty dollars so you can go out and buy those basketball shoes. When you pay back the loan in full, you can have your Nintendo back. How long do you think it'll take you to earn a hundred and twenty bucks?"

"... I could mow lawns. I could wash cars. Um, I guess about six weeks."

"It's a deal," Mom says. "You give us your Nintendo, we'll loan you one hundred and twenty dollars for six weeks, and you get your basketball shoes right away. Pay us back the loan, and you'll get back your Nintendo."

"Can I play with it while it's ... *collateral?*" the boy asks, trying out the unfamiliar (and unwelcome) word.

"That's the whole point," Dad says. "In our family, when you collateralize something as the basis of a loan, you don't have access to it. Are you clear on the terms? Do we have a deal?"

The idea of mowing lawns and washing cars for six weeks doesn't sound all that fulfilling to the boy, but he really wants those basketball shoes. "Deal," he finally says.

This story has a happy ending. Dad agreed to help his son out by passing out flyers at work offering his son's after-school car wash services, and he also lined up some lawns for his son to mow. Dad further agreed to contribute fifty cents to every dollar the young man raised. The boy earned his one hundred and twenty dollars in less than a month. Ironically, he never felt the urge to play with his beloved Nintendo the whole time he was paying off the loan. Even after he earned it back, he never took it out of the box. Instead, a few months later, he sold it to a friend, and put the proceeds toward the purchase of an XBox™, which he "absolutely had to have."

Which quadrants were affected by this experience? The obvious is the Financial. He earned the money so he could have the shoes he desired. The Core Asset value increased because he experienced the discipline and satisfaction of hard work. Of course, the Experience Quadrant increased, because the son had banked this experience. He knows he can do it again and probably more. His confidence increased dramatically. And the Contribution Quadrant benefited, because Dad demonstrated the power of rewarding others when they seek to help themselves.

Whether we're talking about the Vanderbilts and Rockefellers or the Joneses down the street, it all comes down to the same issue: The transfer of wealth without accountability leads to trouble. We deprive our children of the opportunity to make their own choices, learn their own lessons, find out who they are and how best to create abundance for themselves and contribute to society. Are you transferring wealth without accountability? How do you transmit more than money to the next generation?

Leaving No Legacy

The third most common fear that affects the affluent is that they will leave no positive legacy. In other words, all their hard work will die when they do.

No one wants to work one's whole life and die without leaving a meaningful legacy. Most people want to believe their lives have made a difference. They want their positive contributions to be remembered and exemplified in the lives of their children and grandchildren. How can we guarantee a legacy of significance that translates into emotionally and financially self-sufficient descendents, if the only thing we (and our advisors) focus on is passing along Financial Assets?

As defined in Chapter 7, addiction is *Never having enough of the things we don't need*. Based on that definition, can we become addicted to the things in our Financial Quadrant?

It seems that we can never have enough in this quadrant. If money were water, people would be posturing to prove who had the biggest lake. We live near a lake called the Great Salt Lake. It is huge, but like the Dead Sea in Israel, water flows in regularly, but not out. Consequently, it stinks at times. There is no flora surrounding the lake, no fish in the water or animals looking for food along the shoreline. It just sits there and stagnates.

To apply Quadrant Living principles is to build rivers of wealth, not lakes. Quadrant Living principles are concerned with securing the flow of the river and remaining confident that enough tributaries exist to insure against stagnation. This river is vibrant, active and life sustaining.

What would happen if financial and estate advisors built "subdivisions"—gated communities of a sort—regulating the flow of financial wealth, instead of creating fixed plans for the accumulation and transfer of wealth.

An illustration of the latter approach follows: You enter through a beautiful, ornate gated entranceway. A smartly uniformed guard salutes as you make your way into the community. As you glance at the mansions that line the streets of this lovely neighborhood, you discover something strange: That house over there doesn't have a roof on it. The house next to it lacks landscaping. That third house has no windows or doors. You step inside a few houses, and find that some lack paint, others lack appliances, a refrigerator or an oven, and none of them has a stick of furniture on which to sit.

In my experience, many financial, estate or "wealth" planners are great at starting things, but it is not uncommon for them to lose focus before the job is finished. Some professionals view their work as transaction-based rather than as an ongoing relationship with their clients. The best financial planners construct the initial plan as the best architects build structures, continually monitoring their clients' needs and making the necessary adjustments when their clients' lives and needs change. Unfortunately, there are few financial planners who "architect" in this manner.

Why are some of these lesser financial and estate planners often financially successful, regardless? What magic do they offer that makes their services so irresistible to those with assets to protect or pass on? It all comes back to the fear of losing choice and control over their financial assets. They desperately want a plan that will help them avoid this.

In addition, many who acquire financial wealth develop a great passion to win the game against paying taxes, both during their lifetime and in their estate planning. This desire to avoid the taxman, now and later, makes them fair game for anyone who fans the flames of their fears and brings "creative" solutions to the never-ending battle with the IRS.

Financial planning, wealth planning, and estate planning each have a place in our lives. Everyone needs to have a financial plan, indeed; but we're talking about something much more important to the health and well-being of you and your family, not just the current generation, but for generations to come. Do we wish to teach our children and grandchildren to eat the fruit without thought of planting seeds for the future?

We were invited to advise one prominent American family, with a name so well known that they could rightly be described as an American institution. We'll call them the "Smiths." They have been wealthy for a long time, and they are still extremely wealthy today.

They had a problem: They couldn't get along. They couldn't figure out how to invest or spend the vast financial resources at their fingertips. In most families, this kind of dispute over financial governance leads to hurt feelings that are often resolved over a relatively short period of time. Not so for the Smiths. When families like the Smiths get out of whack, they call in lawyers. Lots and lots of lawyers—legions of lawyers!

Somewhere along the line, in between all the legal skirmishes (which were getting them nowhere), they called in our Quadrant Living team to conduct a family retreat.

The weekend with the Smiths was long and difficult. These were people who hadn't just agreed to disagree; they had agreed to despise one another, and to make it impossible for each other to benefit from the enormous wealth they shared. This family was in dire need of an intervention, and it fell on a colleague of mine to mediate their vast differences of opinions and attitudes.

The first thing he did was to seek to clear the air, which had an electricity similar to what you experience just before a late-afternoon thunderstorm on a sultry summer day.

As they went around the room, each family member was encouraged to say, "I feel like saying ..." as a preface, and then adding anything at all about the way they felt about other family members present. Others were not allowed to argue: "Yeah, but—" or "You're wrong" was not an option. Each Smith had the responsibility to make a statement that did not shame or blame the others.

For example, it was okay to say, "I feel like saying that when my father did such-and-such, it made me feel [fill in the blank]."

The Smiths were asked to refrain from saying shaming statements, and the listeners were asked to respond with silence. As each person concluded speaking, the listeners were asked to only respond with, "Thank you for sharing." This continued until everyone had a chance to say everything they wanted to say.

The family members, to their credit, were willing to play along, and more important, they were willing to play by the rules. They stuck to remarks that may have induced guilt, but certainly were not intended to create shame. As I mentioned earlier in Chapter 10, there's an important distinction between guilt and shame: Guilt occurs when we feel badly about something we have done. Is guilt a good thing or a bad thing? I think that depends. Try and imagine a world without guilt. Guilt can be a motivating tool to recognize what we may have done wrong, and to think about how best to remedy those situations or avoid them in the future. Remember, shame, by contrast, occurs when we feel bad about *who we are.* Shame accomplishes nothing other than compounding emotional pain.

Why did we go through this exercise? It's very hard for people to agree when they covertly hold unexpressed feelings which border on hatred for each other. These negative feelings, some of which may have been stewing for decades, must be aired before any real progress is made.

Once the feelings were on the table, they were able to work through them; then, for at least a short while, they moved past them. Over the course of the weekend, the Smiths ultimately agreed to two simple statements that expressed their family's philosophy: "Family first" and "Together we're better."

You might think that a family retreat with a paid moderator is going to great lengths to agree on two such obvious statements, but the Smiths are not your average divisive family. Being able to agree on those two statements in a single weekend was, in their opinion, nothing short of miraculous.

The Smiths still had a long way to go, however, in establishing rules of family governance, decision-making procedures, and getting along without constantly resorting to legal help. But they had made a beginning.

I sometimes hear families say, "Lee, we'd like to have a stronger family connection, but we just aren't on the same page. Do you really think you can help us?"

If it doesn't require the services of a dozen of America's leading (and most expensive) Trust and Estate law firms to get your family to sit down to a Thanksgiving dinner, you're *way* ahead of the Smiths.

Family Leadership

The Brower Quadrant philosophy can help any family, but real progress takes place when there is willingness from the older generation in a family to lead in a productive, proactive manner. You don't need all of your family members on board initially. Some may take a little time to come around; that is human nature. But if they see that you have something exciting brewing, something from which they will benefit as individuals and as members of the family, it's only a matter of time before they will want to join in.

Not every family is receptive to this harmony and cohesion. In some families, a patriarch or matriarch takes an authoritarian stance: "You'll find out what estate planning I've done after I die."

In such instances, wealth may be a means of controlling the family, pitting family members against one another, and generally "running the show" to the detriment of the emotional lives of all. It happens all the time. Ironically, the "estate planning" to which such autocratic heads of the family refer is, more often than not, nonexistent. In many cases, the relative who most benefits from all of that individual's hard work is Uncle Sam!

I believe an industry transformation is emerging. Individuals and families need a more customized approach in the financial services industry. You will begin to see pronounced differences in the delivery of estate planning solutions. They will be customized to include all of a family's true wealth. Dan Sullivan, founder and president of Strategic Coach, has more than thirty years of experience coaching more than two thousand professionals in the financial services industry and has a following of another ten thousand professionals. Dan's predictions of the evolution of the financial services industry over the next twenty-five years are:

- The financial services industry will increasingly become the target of lawsuits.

- Attorneys will increasingly govern the marketing policies, practices and activities of financial services.

- Every product and service of financial services will become increasingly commoditized.

- Because of commoditization fees and commissions paid for product and service, sales will steadily decline.

- The complexity and cost of being a commoditized financial advisor will steadily increase.

- Financial advisors will increasingly be forced to make a career decision—leave the industry, become a salaried employee or become a privately branded entrepreneur.

- Financial advisors, through their unique processes, will innovate more fundamental solutions to economic, political and social issues.

- The entire financial services industry will be transformed and improved through innovative financial advisors.

Buckminster Fuller stated that the surest way to extinction is through over-specialization. Those who thrive need a steward to guide them through the flood of information available—an unbiased, comprehensive advisor who stays current in many different specialties and professions, just like an architect. He or she has to know which experts are the best in their particular specialty. When creating plans for a bridge or a building, a good architect realizes the most important step is *thoroughly understanding and being in harmony with the vision of the client.* We see the creation of an entirely new approach to estate planning.

This new approach, and the cadre of financial experts who administer it, is rooted in the Brower Quadrant philosophy. Money need not tear families apart. Family leadership is a method used by families to create and *empower* their Family Quadrant Bank—a system in which families gain in strength and wisdom, instead of setting themselves up for destruction and the dissipation of wealth in all quadrants.

Remember, you want to find an advisor who shares your values, one who focuses on the assets found in your Core, Experience, and Contribution Asset quadrants as well as the Financial, and has the systems to perpetuate that wealth into and for the benefit of future generations.

Leadership Versus Management

The concepts of management and leadership are often confused. I equate reactivity with management and proactivity with leadership. Leaders set the vision. Management carries it out. You can have management without leadership and you end up with more activity than long term results. You cannot have leadership without management. Good managers demand results now. Leaders invest in systems that will create greater results over the long term. Management makes sure that tasks are completed, boxes get checked off and to-do lists get handled. It's easy to become a prisoner of a to-do list—it happens to each of us practically every day. Management of our time simply means checking off the maximum number of tasks in a minimum number of minutes. Not much excitement there! Managing others entails a similar approach: trying to find ways to motivate people to clean out their in-boxes. Indeed, this will get chores done, but when we manage either our own responsibilities or other people's, are we sharing with them a vision? Doubtful. In my experience, protecting and sharing the vision, is the most important responsibility of a leader. Great leaders have a unique team that sets out the systems and methods to achieve the vision.

Because of the Internet and entrepreneurism, management in the world has never been so studied and prolific. We see entrepreneurial consultants who have micro-analyzed every aspect of management. The Internet provides more tools to increase management skills. Political leaders analyze what they should say and to whom to say it to get re-elected. Management within publicly held companies knows exactly how to utilize the volumes of data to match shareholders and public opinion with what they need to keep their job and command such huge salaries and other incentives. Has the world become great managers at the expense of leadership? Do political leaders focus more on their constituencies and the short term objective to get themselves or their party elected? Are they leading or managing the opinions of those that vote for them?

Are we seeing similar patterns within the family? Have we become phenomenal managers at home at the expense of family leadership? It's amazing the management skills that parents master to accommodate their children. Have we become expert "soccer moms and dads" hauling our kids here and there, setting out rules that "protect" our children from disappointment and making sure they keep up with what everyone else is doing? And the children still get bored.

Consider the Motion Picture Rating Association, inaugurated in the 1970s to help parents "manage" what their children view. Now, when teenagers announce that they are going to the movies, the typical first or second question is, "What is it rated?" That is a management question.

Have you ever been sitting in the movie theatre with your spouse and you lean over and ask, "What is this rated? Is this really only PG-13? Do you think the children have seen this?" Let's look at the basic ingredients of leadership.

The Five C's of True Leadership

Clarity: Leadership involves creating a vision for ourselves and sharing that vision with those around us, whether our sphere of influence is our family, workplace or a nation. Leadership is about developing, sharing and sustaining the vision. Leaders are visionary. They establish, hone and restate the vision frequently to ensure a clear understanding and that it leads the way to achieve that vision. Continuous clarity cemented in gratitude always increases energy, enthusiasm, camaraderie and determination for those who share the vision. Does each member of your family understand the collective vision or purpose of your family?

Consciousness: A leader is aware of the bond between every member of the universe and the richness of the earth they share. A leader is neither an optimist nor a pessimist. I define a pessimist as one who believes the world to be rapidly degenerating to self-serving materialism and looks to the past for pleasure. An optimist, on the other hand, ignores the present and looks to the future for happiness. A leader looks at a glass that is filled to the midpoint with water. Rather than saying the glass is half empty or half full, the leader responds that it is full. The glass is full of water and air and we need both to survive. A leader is content in the present time, motivated by the future and enriched with confidence from the past, while focusing in the present. A leader teaches and inspires others to learn wisdom from the past, embrace the vision of the future, and live and perform now. We own our past and we can own our future. The present represents what we have learned from the past, the inspiration of our vision of the future; however, our choices and actions can only happen now and determine our future.

Consistency: A leader is consistent and will not compromise the long term vision for short term results. Obstacles are the raw material provided for discovering solutions, rather than impediments that force a leader off path. A leader understands that it is more important to be respected than admired, never compromises integrity and is predictable when it comes to commitment and values. Children, spouse, employees and team members can fully rely on this leader. One responsibility we cannot evade is our influence. No individual is so insignificant as to be without influence. Leaders take this responsibility a step further, becoming not being merely an influence, but also an inspiration.

Courage: A leader has courage, which is often the antithesis of conformity. A leader's objective is to consciously train the mind and body to act unconsciously in support of the group or family's values and vision. In a sense, the leader is a parent who understands that children (or team members) need role models, discipline and guidance—not simply another friend. A leader knows to make corrections along the journey, and have the courage to do so, never taking an eye off the vision. Courage is synonymous with character, which is the ability to carry out a worthwhile decision once the emotion of making that decision has passed.

Compassion: A leader does not force anyone to change, but rather, allows each person's unique ability to surface in a safe environment. Leaders do not lay blame, justify or participate in shaming themselves or others. Instead, in difficult situations, mistakes are regarded as learning opportunities, and leaders look to the system for solutions. Greater success is achieved when leaders ask, "What worked? How can we do more of that?" Rather than critically identifying and focusing on what didn't work, individuality is honored and everyone is appreciated.

These attributes of true leaders are just as valid at home as in the workplace. We're often great managers of our children. We manage their increasingly complex schedules, shuttling them from track practice to violin lessons to French class. We manage their lives, from finding the right nursery school to supervising their college application process. We have a right to feel good about ourselves for the things we do as parents—attend parent/teacher conferences and show up for our children in every way possible. The danger of being merely managers, however, is that we may give our children a vision of life as an endless to-do list, rather than guiding them to a vision of life that is ultimately about who they *are*, and not just about what they *do*.

Moving from management to leadership—from reactivity to proactivity—may sound intimidating, but it doesn't have to be. It comes back to the fundamental principle that all progress begins by telling the truth. When we tell ourselves the truth about where we are, we take our first steps toward clarity, allowing us to create and sustain a vision, to which we can confidently lead others.

What have you done to ensure your Financial Assets will be allocated as you desire upon your passing?

What small steps can you take to ensure this in the days, weeks and months that follow?

Additional questions for families:

How have you handled requests from your children when they wished to use the Financial Assets in an Empowered Q-Bank?

How might you do this differently in the future?

Further reflection:

Are you transferring wealth without accountability?

List ways in which you might transfer more than money to the next generation?

chapter 14

who owns your future?

We are stewards of this abundance, and with stewardship, comes both responsibility and opportunity.

Is your future an asset or a liability? We discussed the value of "owning" your past when we explored the assets in your Experience quadrant. When you *own* your past, you take responsibility for your experiences, good and bad, and you learn from them. They then become assets available for future withdrawal.

Unlike activity in your financial quadrant, any activity— a deposit or a withdrawal—increases the value of your Experience Asset account. (This is also your Wisdom account.) As long you continue to learn and share your knowledge, you increase the value of your Q-Bank.

If you can take ownership of your past and deposit it as an asset into your family bank, would the same be true of your future? Can your future be an asset? Absolutely! Unfortunately, there are those who wander aimlessly in the present, blaming their woes on the past, and so overcome with perceived barriers to their future dreams that they do, in fact, unknowingly write the script of their future. They are paralyzed by either the finality of the past or the fear and uncertainty of the future. How we spend our time each day is either a deposit or withdrawal from our future—every choice we make, every thought, every action. The key is to have Quadrant Motion. How do you achieve and maintain Quadrant Motion? There are seven important steps to help you "own" your future, which increase levels of productivity, peace and joy for you, your family, community and business.

Follow these steps and you will accomplish more with less effort, faster.

The Seven Steps of Quadrant Motion

One: Rock It!

Everything begins with gratitude. Gratitude, however, is a learned attribute. It must be practiced. It does not always come naturally. Think of a newborn baby. If she could talk, do you think her first words would be "Thank you"? No, they would most likely be "Feed me." My system to maintain focus on gratitude is to carry my gratitude rock with me as a reminder of the blessings and abundance in my life.

Someone who feels they have not received what they deserve experiences a lack of gratitude. When we live in gratitude, we are better prepared to learn, receive and grow. Nothing prepares you to take charge of your life and activate the law of attraction like gratitude.

As I began to accumulate a meaningful level of financial wealth I asked myself; "What is my stewardship responsibility to wealth and when does it end?" Am I a steward over *all* of my assets or just my Financial Assets?

Yes, I am a steward over all of my assets, and no, that stewardship never ends. Stewardship is powerless without gratitude. The very idea of stewardship has become an asset for me; I would like it to be an asset for my family and generations to come. Ask yourself this question: What is my stewardship responsibility to my True Wealth today?

Going through the motions each day without an awareness of the gifts of abundance with which we all are so lovingly blessed intensifies an attitude of scarcity, making it that much more difficult to see and appreciate those gifts. It is virtually impossible to attract what we need when we focus on what we don't have. We are stewards of this abundance, and with stewardship comes both responsibility and opportunity.

Awareness allows gratitude, and gratitude brings more awareness. Awareness means being present in this moment, unencumbered by fear, worry and resentment. Being present clears the senses and allows us to see the abundant opportunities and relationships that are available to us.

Unfortunately, we live in a world governed by a fear of scarcity. I believe our responsibility, now more than ever, is to counteract the deluge of negativity and growing fears of scarcity that surround us every day. We must find new ways to think about our lives, rather than unconsciously drink from the contaminated waters of negativity, which pollute our very cells, the fiber of our "being".

With a multitude of great complainers—media, politicians, educators, friends, neighbors and, yes, even family—offering hefty servings of negativity, we can slowly find ourselves poisoned by the deluge of petty grievances and pessimistic observations if we are not careful. Worse yet, once poisoned, we become polluters, unknowingly spraying our critical waters on the heads of those around us—our family, friends and co-workers.

As leaders, we have a responsibility to purify those waters, for ourselves and for others. We can begin to transform negative influences, first within ourselves and then for those whom we love most. Many others will be constructively influenced as a result. Imagine a world of those who encourage and provide solutions rather than offering discouragement and complaints. Leaders inspire with gratitude and develop solutions using positive creativity. Creativity and negativity cannot occupy the same space at the same time, any more than light can occupy the same space with darkness.

Gratitude is the attitude, the condition, the world, the vista, the habit, the power, the motivator, the activator, the stabilizer and the soil that nurtures your vision. Gratitude engenders appreciation. Appreciation begets value. Gratitude + Appreciation = Increasing Value!

If gratitude is the noun, appreciation is the verb and increased value is the direct object. Investors love appreciation. Homeowners love appreciation. Collectors love appreciation. You love appreciation. Fellow employees love appreciation. Your family thrives on appreciation. When you appreciate someone or something, the value of that person or object increases in value, like investment portfolios, real estate and art. Do you want to increase the value of your relationship with your spouse and your children? First, be grateful for who they are—right now, at this very moment—not what you want or expect them to be. Acknowledge that appreciation by recognizing them through kind words and actions. Their value and esteem will automatically surge, as will yours.

As mentioned earlier, I use a Gratitude Rock as a system to keep me present and "grounded." From this space of grounded gratitude, I become an attractant. And so will you. You will attract great relationships—relationships that are attracted to you and your vision. You will attract phenomenal opportunities, those that will open doors and lead you on new and exciting pathways to your grandest visions. Gratitude is the lubricant that eliminates the wear and tear of daily trials and frustrations. Don't let anyone take that away from you. Treasure it!

I was recently in a long slow line at a drive-thru restaurant. Not wanting to waste time, I began reading a book I had with me. Suddenly, I heard a "honk, honk" from behind me. I looked in my rearview mirror and beheld a thirty-something business person in a shirt and tie, sunglasses, cell phone against his left ear, his right hand in the air, palm up, looking at me like I must be an idiot for not advancing the one car-length that had opened up in front of me. I almost reverted to my old behavior. Then, I remembered the rock in my pocket and why I carry it. I did not want to lose the power of gratitude. When I got to the window, I paid for the car behind me. I am not sure what it did for him; I know how it affected me: It allowed me to stay in a space of "positive" energy. I was in control of how I felt, and I did not intend to give that control away.

You have the power to create the perfect conditions to achieve your visions, the power to move your "True Wealth" through generations, impacting thousands, if not millions, of lives. Live in gratitude! Rock on!

Two: Think It!

Thought precedes action, whether the result is a miracle or a tragedy. Conscious thought makes a deposit into the subconscious that ultimately exhibits itself in action. Some people live in the future in an effort to "own" their future. They are dreamers. They either live in a kind of "la-la" land, or worse, they are constantly bringing tomorrow's clouds over to today. Remember, you have the choice to determine whether your future is a liability or an asset. We gain wisdom from the past, establish our vision in the future and make it happen in the present. Our thoughts may be of the past or of the future, but they happen now. Think it! Support your subconscious mind with positive thoughts and experiences. Remember, our objective is to consciously train the mind and body to act unconsciously in support of the vision and values of our family or business.

When growing up, I had the privilege to watch one of the great baseball players of all time—Willie Mays. Today, long-time baseball enthusiasts still talk about "The Catch." "The Catch" refers to a dazzling defensive play made by Mays, the New York Giants' centerfielder, on a line drive by the Cleveland Indians' Vic Wertz, more than 460 feet from home plate at New York's Polo Grounds to save Game 1 of the 1954 World Series. With the score tied at 2-2, the Indians had runners on first and second base and were threatening to pull ahead for the win. Wertz hit the ball right on the seams, a long soaring line drive to dead centerfield.

Mays got a perfect jump on the ball. Some accounts claim that before the ball had even made contact with the bat, Mays turned around, and with his head down and his back to the plate, sprinted more than 100 feet to the deepest part of the ballpark. At the last moment, on a dead run away from home plate, Mays put his glove up and made a two-handed, over-the-shoulder catch, an estimated 462 feet from the plate. As amazing as the catch was, Mays made an even more amazing play on the throw back to the infield to save the run. As he made the catch, he slammed on the brakes, whirled and fired a no-look bullet to second base to prevent a run.

I'm convinced Mays knew he was going to make the catch before he made it and was already starting the next phase of the play as he squeezed the ball into his glove. Imagine if Mays would have had to consciously compute all of the calculations that would put him in exactly the right spot as the ball hit 462 feet from the plate. He would have had to calculate the weight of the ball, the speed of the pitch, the weight and substance of the bat, the trajectory of the swing, the weight and strength of the batter, the temperature and humidity and much more. What happened? The unconscious mind took over. In such a situation, the unconscious mind clearly outperforms the conscious mind.

The choices we make *make* us. We can decide right now that all of our choices and actions will be deposits into our Experience Asset quadrant, which we can then withdraw as needed in the future. It begins with consciously training your unconscious mind. Conscious thought eventually becomes unconscious action.

Three: See It!

You can't just think your vision—you must see it. A vision is the representation of your most important thoughts, dreams and intentions. It is unique to you. Only you have it. Feel it. Own it. It is a mental construct of your future. As a leader in your home, your workplace and in the community, it is your job to share this vision. Like the horizon, as you move towards it, it will move as well. You cannot reach the horizon. You can't sneak up on it. But you *can* move it.

A leader's vision is what sustains him and those that follow through the tough times and through the times of incredible success. It is what keeps you grounded, focused and in motion. Years ago, a very successful entrepreneur shared the following story:

He loved to do high mountain hiking—not technical climbing—but hiking trails at extreme altitude. One particular afternoon, he was trekking at about 13,000 feet in Colorado. There were about four inches of snow on the ground and he struggled with each breath as he drudgingly placed one foot in front of the other. Unexpectedly, he could hear another person on the trail coming from behind. He said when that happens, his instinct is to quicken his pace—can't afford to look too slow. Eventually this fellow hiker began to pass him. As he looked to his left, here was this man in his seventies, determined and marching at a steady pace that was obviously faster than my friend could muster.

Before he was out of arms' length, my friend reached out and touched his arm. "What drives you?" he gasped. Then these profound words were uttered by the older gentleman:

"My vision of the future sustains my present agonies."

And then he continued on, leaving my friend to ponder this powerful phrase.

I have thought about this many times since he shared this story. Isn't it our vision of the future that inspires, motivates and sustains us and those that accompany or follow us?

In Chapter 8, you went through the Quadrant Clarity Experience. You concluded this exercise by writing your three-year vision statement. This is your current horizon; it is for the benefit of you and your family. In order to succeed with your vision, you must visit it frequently—as often as possible.

I have found a great friend in meditation. I resisted this for years. I thought meditation was for "kooks." I could not see myself sitting around in some weird pose humming and mellowing out. It did not seem to be my nature. Then a good friend of mine, Paul Scheele of Learning

Strategies Inc., convinced me to give it a try. Next to prayer, meditation has become the single most powerful daily activity I can recommend for anyone. If you are not familiar with meditation, I encourage you to begin with guided meditation. Paul has a series called "Sonic Access" that I especially like because it combines several of the most advanced techniques of meditation and brain training in one experience. I end each session more energized and with greater clarity for the day to move me toward my vision.

Visualization has become so integral to my life that I often pray without using any words. I picture in my mind's eye all that I am grateful for. Then, rather than ask for anything, I simply visualize outcomes. I see my children smiling, healthy and appreciative. I feel the strong and magical relationship with my wife Lori, and see us together. I visualize those I work with productive, healthy and happy. Try it. It is a gratifying experience. Visualize the people, experiences and things for which you are grateful. Clearly envision the blessings you desire for yourself and others. If you are praying for the health of a loved one, for example, you don't need to express your desire in words. Picture them healthy, happy and productive. At the end of this prayer, I feel energized.

The power of thought, coupled with vision, is an essential step in attracting your most amazing dreams, but it's not all you need. You also need to take the first step.

Four: Move It!

Get in motion! Full of gratitude, with thoughts of abundance, and a precise unclouded vision, you are fully prepared to get into motion. Many times the first steps are awkward. Think of little babies learning to walk; they don't jump up running. They take little baby steps, and if the babies are lucky, parents encourage, encourage, and encourage them! This is what you want to do for yourself. Provide love, support and a safe environment for error and learning. Babies must keep trying over and over until they "get it." Not "getting it" is part of the learning process. Once babies "get it," they are off. They do not lie in their cribs thinking, "Someday, I am going to walk with the best of them." They get in motion—then the miracles happen, but not until then.

What does it take to get a ship in motion? You merely have to lift the anchor. How high do you have to lift the anchor to get into motion? Lift it just an inch and with the slightest wind or waves it will begin to move. Motion is as important to your success as is gratitude, thought and vision. You must move—sometimes, even before your vision is crystal clear. And, just like a little baby, it probably will feel awkward at first. True progress always requires that you leave your comfort zone. Take small steps. "Pringle" it. Once in motion, magic can happen. The Law of Attraction begins to work for you. The Law of Attraction can then combine with the Law of Precession to harmoniously and exponentially propel you beyond your current horizon. This is very exciting.

I first became aware of the Law of Precession when I was introduced to the teachings of Buckminster Fuller. Fuller stated that precession is a primary means of system inter-connection. "Precession is the effect of bodies in motion on other bodies in motion. And all Universe is a complex of bodies in motion, so all the inter-effects are preces-sional." Bucky said that precessional effects are what most people label "side effects," i.e., I teach a person to fish so he can feed his family (direct effect). One of his no longer hungry children now can focus in school and goes on to become an important scientist (precessional effect).

Precession in nature always occurs at right angles or ninety degrees to the initial activity. Take, for exam-ple, the simple honey bee. The bee gets in motion. If he just sat around and thought about having nectar for the queen, the queen would starve. He leaves the hive search-ing for luscious fields of beautiful nectar filled flowers. In his quest to be the star bee, what happens? His feet and wings become covered with pollen and he contributes to the pollination of fruits and vegetables throughout the world. Did the bee have a vision? Yes, he desired nectar. Did he act on it? Yes, he got the nectar. But his act of motion creates even greater, more dramatic results.

The bee did not intend to pollinate, yet he does so and benefits both systems. The bee's presence on a flower with the appropriate structure transfers pollen to the bee. He is seeking energy (nectar) and finds it in a flower. The energy required for the pollen contact is not part of the intentional action and reaction, which is the bee gathering nectar. It is excess energy from the bee's physical contact that provides the possible pathway for the pollen to be gathered and shared. The flower has excess energy in the form of pollen. Instead of waiting for wind to distribute it to another flower, the bee is an agent that can couple to this energy.

On May 25, 1961, President John F. Kennedy, in a speech to Congress, declared, *"I believe that this nation should commit itself to achieving the goal, before this decade is out, of landing a man on the moon and returning him safely to the earth. No single space project in this period will be more impressive to mankind or more important for the long-range exploration of space, and none will be so difficult or expensive to accomplish."*

Did President Kennedy, as the leader of The United States of America, establish the vision? In NASA folklore, there is a story of a congressman visiting Cape Canaveral during a time when he was trying to make up his mind on whether to fund the Apollo project. In the men's restroom was a janitor who was obviously proud of the very clean facility he maintained. When asked by the congressman why he was inspired to do such a magnificent job, the humble worker proudly replied that he was part of the team that was going to put a man on the moon and bring him home! Did a whole nation rise up and accept the challenge united in that vision and did they get into motion?

And what are all of the precessional opportunities, relationships and experiences that sprang from getting into motion? I can think of a few: Velcro, Tang, computer miniaturization and literally thousands of other inventions which created thousands of untold numbers of jobs and millions of dollars of revenue.

Can you think of how precession impacts your life? By being in motion, even with just baby steps, you engage the intertwining laws of attraction and precession. Imagine if bees were entrepreneurs. By being aware of how these laws work, they could make a fortune on the precessional affects of their honey making efforts. Now that you know how these laws work, you can live them and you can share them.

When you are grounded in a positive attitude, your vision is fresh and vibrant. You get into motion and stay present to these laws. Your milestones will be your former horizons and new and greater horizons will appear before you.

Five: Be It!

To "be it" is about *becoming*. Becoming requires balance in the four quadrants of your life, and that balance requires attention. Do you find it challenging when perceived urgencies and the obligations of day-to-day living cause you to focus on one quadrant to the exclusion of the others? You are not alone.

When doing the Napkin Presentation of the Brower Quadrants, I often ask those in attendance if they would be willing to trade family, health or their values for more money. The answer is always a resounding, "No!" Yet, unfortunately, many do just that every day. When you justify that it's okay to focus on only one quadrant (for example, you may want to receive money more quickly, which will enrich the other quadrants), you give false permission to exclude the other quadrants.

I was a victim of this very thinking. My dad grew up a product of the Depression. His father was quite ill and his mother worked overtime to provide the five children with basic necessities. My father, by his own admission, was a workaholic. He built a small produce business. He left the house before daylight and returned after dusk. Rarely did any of us spend much time with him. When I was old enough to work with him, I began to learn from him. Nobody could outwork him, and his honesty was, and still is, impeccable. Although I am eternally grateful for what he did teach me, I knew him best as a businessman and a worker, and I missed the camaraderie, love and guidance of a father.

I swore I would be different, and I was. I coached my kids, took them on trips, and went to athletic and school events. I realize now, however, that much of this was done while talking on the phone or rushing to get to my next appointment. I was physically present, but it was sometimes difficult to tell where my attention was. I felt that by working harder, I could make enough money so that I could spend "quality" time with my kids. One day, I woke up. I was in my forties and my kids were growing older much faster than I thought possible. I suddenly realized that I was just like my father. I was putting the *essential* at the mercy of the *important*! I was trading quality family time and my health to get more money, so that in the future I could have more quality time with my children. I was doing the wrong thing for the right reason.

Balance does not mean that you must spend equal time in each of the quadrants. It means that you give harmony to each quadrant daily. A great symphony understands the power of the perfect harmonization of each musical section. When attention is focused on only one segment, the entire symphony suffers.

Recently, a good friend called and asked for a favor. A friend of his was living with cancer and was about to undergo major surgery. His friend had recently read the book *The Secret*, and had adopted the system of carrying a Gratitude Rock. He felt a call from me would really cheer her up. I did call her and we had a wonderful conversation. She told me in great detail about her cancer and all that she was learning and doing. She was very focused on getting well—as she should be. She then expressed her worry and fear, which, too, is very understandable. I asked her what she was doing for others. There was a long pause, and then, an emotional response.

"Nothing. I am so focused on me and my cancer, I haven't made time to focus on others."

Our engaging discussion moved to talk about balance and how balance eliminates "the wobble" mentioned at the beginning of this book. It is difficult to give one hundred percent when we have a wobble. Our thoughts can't give us unanimous support if we feel even a little deficient in the other quadrants. Attention on being "whole" and healthy will be better focused and much more effective when we first eliminate the wobble. My friend called me the next day and told me she had invited him to lunch.

"What did you say to her?" he asked. "She took me to a drive-thru restaurant and paid for the car behind us!"

Attend to each quadrant every day, even if it is only to acknowledge appreciation of your assets. Doing this will eliminate recurring "wobbles" and permit you to bestow greater attention to the activities you need to focus on right now. Again, this does not mean you must spend *equal* time in the Core, Experience, Contribution and Financial quadrants, but it is important to dedicate *some* time to each one. Allow all aspects of your life to find harmony with each other. You will attract and achieve more. Each morning, ask yourself:

What small step can I take today to increase the value in each quadrant of my life?

What can I do today for my individual, health, happiness and well-being?

What small step can I take to develop a new skill, strengthen a relationship or acquire new learning today?

What can I do for others today?

What small step can I do to enrich or empower my Financial Assets today?

Think in terms of very small steps. How far do you have to lift the anchor for the boat to get into motion? Just lift the anchor an inch and see what happens. This small but significant investment will give you a return of speed, efficiency and peace of mind.

Six: Capture It!

Capturing our assets is a key concept of the Brower Quadrant. *Capture* is an essential ingredient for optimizing assets. The optimization of assets is the process (or the "system") of creating multiple lives for all of our assets—not Financial Assets alone. When we optimize our assets we convert them to capital.

Capitalizing our Financial Assets is a common practice. You can fly into any city in the U.S., and in a matter of days (sometimes hours), you could select a property, negotiate a price, obtain clear title, wire the money and close on the property. Within days of that transaction, you could leverage that title with a bank and add another property to your Financial Assets. You have taken one asset and capitalized it by acquiring another piece of real estate.

Hernando de Soto, in his book *The Mystery of Capital,* illustrates this concept utilizing a mountain lake. A mountain lake can serve the purpose of providing recreation, solitude; perhaps water sports or vacation experiences. An engineer, however, might look at it differently. By building a dam at one end of the lake, the engineer would be able to preserve the original purpose of the lake—a refuge of vacation homes and recreation-while creating a new life (purpose) of generating electricity for towns in the surrounding area.

Our experiences are much the same. If we harness (capture) the experience and then transform what worked about that experience into a system or process (optimize), we have made a deposit into our Q-Bank. It has a life of its own that will benefit others long after our lives have ended. The celebration and transformation of our experiences is essential to our progress and the speed at which it occurs. We capture our experiences by celebrating and sharing them, and we optimize them by transforming them into systems from which we can withdraw whenever necessary. The tradition of sharing our positive experiences at work with clients and co-workers, and at home with family members, is a prime example of how we can capture life's experiences.

Seven: Shift It!

You are now ready to shift into a new and more powerful gear. You cannot successfully shift into the highest gear without going through the other gears first; meaning, you cannot move into step seven of the Quadrant Motion Theory without going through steps one through six first.

Let's assume you have done this in the course of reading this book. Thus, you are in balanced motion, moving with an attitude of abundance and gratitude, firmly focused on your vision and depositing into your family Q-Bank the value from each experience, opportunity and relationship. What happens with your confidence? It quietly begins to soar. Like attracts like. When you exude a sense of purpose that rivals earth's gravity, you draw to you even greater relationships and opportunities.

You will reach new heights with this burgeoning confidence. It gives you a new perspective of who you are and what you are capable of accomplishing. You will see a new horizon, which generates deep appreciation for where you have been, where you are now and where you have the potential of going. This leads to new thoughts, new vision and new motion, as you continue to balance your approach and capture your progress as you go.

chapter 15

the essence of the brower quadrant

"Family is a quilt, one generation stitched to the next, and gratitude for each other is the thread that holds us together."

Noah benShea

Great theories lead to reliable systems. To achieve fulfillment of life's purpose, one must implement true principles with self, extend them to family and then create systems that empower those who follow. The Brower Quadrant embraces *gratitude* and its power to attract positive circumstances, treasures and achieves purpose through *leadership*, empowers wisdom through *legacy*, and optimizes the four categories of assets through *leverage*.

Gratitude is a divine power that supports all of the laws of attraction known to man. Don't you just love being around people who sincerely live in gratitude? They inspire and they attract. They attract greater opportunities and greater relationships in their lives. Do you enjoy being around people who do not express gratitude? They actually repel great opportunities and relationships. They may experience short-term achievements; however, it will not last. Which are you? Are you truly living in gratitude? Are you attracting those opportunities and relationships that will cause you to grow and succeed?

When you consider that less than 4% of family wealth survives beyond the fourth generation, you have to admit that traditional "estate planning" has failed. Those families who have implemented systems of gratitude within their personal lives, their family lives and their business lives, attract abundance. Children who learn and live gratitude are more open to learning, growing and contributing. They are healthier, happier and have greater self-esteem. And others are more open to share what they know and what they possess with them. Begin now, living and sharing systems of gratitude.

You can start by sharing positive experiences at dinner or opening each business meeting with a Positive Focus. Not surprisingly, you will run into opposition. There is no shortage of negative energy. There are those who will oppose you and cause you to doubt yourself. Don't stop! The world needs your positive energy. It is contagious. And true leaders will be consistent! Adopt a Gratitude Rock. Use it to remind yourself of the abundance in your life, and to appreciate the challenges as well as the opportunities for what you learn from them. I receive e-mails almost daily from people around the world sharing stories of gratitude inspired by keeping a rock in their pocket.

Leadership is an endangered species. The world has become more focused on immediate gratification than on long-term results and sustainability. This "have now, pay later" disease has infected our politicians, our business leaders, our communities, our educational institutions and yes, even our families. If we don't eliminate this disease, it could lead to a total collapse of everything that we truly value. Leadership is sustained by a leader's long-term vision and ability to engage those who surround him/her in the process of protecting and surpassing that vision.

The industry I represent, the cottage industry of Estate Planning, has fallen victim to the short-term goal of avoiding taxes and divvying up the assets equally among often times ill-prepared heirs. There is a movement afoot to eliminate the term *estate planning*. Estate planning may relate to the legal documents that support a tax-wise method of dividing up the financial assets. However, it is a myth that by completing legal documents, we have both honored the stewardship to our wealth and created a system to protect and perpetuate that wealth for more than one or two generations. When people begin their estate planning, they often do so with the notion that once the legal documents are signed, dated and notarized, the process is complete. Nothing could be further from the truth. Estate planning is an ongoing process that involves more than trusts that run the risk of becoming out dated. It is *family leadership*—guiding the family through the opportunities of inheriting wisdom, values, traditions, relationships, spirituality, knowledge and the self-esteem that comes from knowing they can make a difference on this planet. This is an ongoing process that cannot ever be "done." What we are really talking about are systems of "Family Leadership."

You can make a difference. You must be a leader. It begins with you and spreads to those you love—and those you influence. Explore the concept of creating your own Empowered Q-Bank that protects and empowers your family's most valuable possessions. This is not difficult. Talk to your advisors. Investigate sources that are familiar with Quadrant Living Systems. That investment will pay you dividends well beyond your lifetime.

Legacy is not merely what you leave behind. Many people believe that a legacy can be purchased. To some it's as simple as having a building named after them. In reality, isn't legacy the positive effect created by our influence that makes life better for those who follow? It is the culmination of the choices we make each day and our ability to capture them for the benefit of those who follow. I am reminded of a poem that is often quoted by my friend Coach John Wooden:

God's Hall of Fame

This crowd on earth
They soon forget
The heroes of the past.
They cheer like mad
Until you fall
And that's how long you last.
But God does not forget,
And in his Hall of Fame,
By just believing in his Son,
Inscribed you'll find your name.

I tell you, friends,
I would not trade
My name however small
Inscribed up there
Beyond the stars
In that celestial hall.

For any famous name on earth
Or glory that they share
I'd rather be an unknown here
And have my name up there.
—*Unknown*

Ask yourself: "What did I (we) do well today and how can I (we) do more of it? What have we learned and how can we make it better for those that follow?" Look for opportunities to "pay it forward." A friendly smile, a tip of the hat, an unexpected compliment or expression of gratitude, anonymously paying for a meal, building your Empowered Q-Bank—are all ways of leaving a legacy.

Leverage is having more—faster and with less effort. When you develop systems of leverage you are able to achieve and influence more in each of the four quadrants of True Wealth. Most people associate the concept of leverage with their financial assets. Marketers constantly bombard us with various forms of the mantra "no money down." Yes, this is the most common form of leverage; however, from a financial point of view, it is the most dangerous. Improper use of leverage puts in peril the underlying supporting assets that are needed to secure our future.

The real question is: "How do I leverage all of my assets— my Core, Experience, Contribution and Financial assets to achieve and influence more, without the risk of losing what I already have?" Systems based upon the Brower Quadrant are designed to help individuals, families and institutions optimize all of their assets for generations to come. Those who implement these systems have a clear vision of the future, and their families and associates are energized by that vision. They are establishing a necessary balance between their desire for financial wealth and their desire for a meaningful life. This balance allows them to focus more on the essential and less on the important.

Leverage also occurs when we unite with a community of individuals who have common interests and values. There is a community developing around Quadrant Living Systems. As we work within the community and share our experiences, good and bad, we will grow even faster. A community has a hub which becomes the axis for an exchange of wisdom. This collective wisdom reduces error and increases predictable outcomes. Sharing means having more! As we continue to grow and to share, the probability for increased success rises dramatically. Together we are better.

As you come to understand the paradigm-breaking tenants of the Brower Quadrant, your mind is opened to new opportunities and challenges. You will begin asking different questions. Different questions lead to different answers and different answers lead to different results. Many people who have been introduced to the Brower Quadrant comment that they wish they had been exposed to it sooner. It's never too late. The impact and simplicity of the Brower Quadrant can make a difference for you and your family right now, regardless of your current situation.

It's never too late.

about the author

Lee Brower, creator of the Quadrant Living system of wealth preservation, has been featured in the best-selling book and movie *The Secret*, and has appeared on *The Today Show*, among other popular programs. The revolutionary new method of financial planning is based on transferring not just monetary wealth, but core assets like health, family and values.

Lee is a noted authority on helping prestigious families create enduring legacies that flourish generation after generation. He is also an accomplished teacher and mentor for entrepreneurs and CEOs. His breakthrough concepts on preserving wealth are changing the landscape of leadership in a variety of places, from private homes and small businesses to public corporations and large educational institutions.

Born and raised in California, Lee attended Brigham Young University and the University of Redlands, where he majored in business administration and Spanish. He then went on to study and practice financial planning, earning a CLU and ChFC designation from American College in Bryn Mawr, Pennsylvania. For more than 10 years, he has served as an Associate Coach for Strategic Coach Inc., an international organization based in Toronto that offers practical-thinking tools and support structures to help individuals create the personal and professional future they want.

Lee resides in the Salt Lake City area with his wife, Lori, where they enjoy the outdoors and the joys that come from having a blended family of eight children and nine grandchildren.